JOSÉ ROBERTO A. IGREJA

What to say when...?

O QUE DIZER EM INGLÊS EM IMPORTANTES
SITUAÇÕES DE COMUNICAÇÃO COTIDIANA

CD de áudio
para melhorar
a compreensão
e ativar a
fluência

© 2015 José Roberto A. Igreja

Preparação de texto: Rosana Martinelli | Verba Editorial

Capa e Projeto Gráfico: Paula Astiz

Editoração Eletrônica: Laura Lotufo | Paula Astiz Design

Ilustrações: Rafael Dourado

Assistente editorial: Aline Naomi Sassaki

CD
Produtora: jm produção de áudio
Locutores: Michael Miller, Rodney Cameron, Sarah Johnson e Shirly Gabay

Dados Internacionais de Catalogação na Publicação (CIP)
(Câmara Brasileira do Livro, SP, Brasil)

Igreja, José Roberto A.
  What to say when...? : o que dizer em inglês em importantes situações de comunicação cotidiana / José Roberto A. Igreja. — Barueri, SP : DISAL, 2015.

  Inclui CD.
  ISBN 978-85-7844-185-2

  1. Inglês – Estudo e ensino 2. Inglês – Expressões idiomáticas 3. Inglês – Vocabulário e manuais de conversação I. Título.

15-07042   CDD-420.7

Índices para catálogo sistemático:
1. Inglês : Estudo e ensino 420.7

Todos os direitos reservados em nome de:
Bantim, Canato e Guazzelli Editora Ltda.

Alameda Mamoré 911 – cj. 107
Alphaville – BARUERI – SP
CEP: 06454-040
Tel. / Fax: (11) 4195-2811
Visite nosso site: www.disaleditora.com.br
Televendas: (11) 3226-3111

Fax gratuito: 0800 7707 105/106
E-mail para pedidos: comercialdisal@disal.com.br

Nenhuma parte desta publicação pode ser reproduzida, arquivada ou transmitida de nenhuma forma ou meio sem permissão expressa e por escrito da Editora.

What to say when...?

SUMÁRIO

9   APRESENTAÇÃO

13   UNIT 1: APRESENTAÇÕES
Apresentando a si próprio e outras pessoas; informações pessoais, vocabulário e expressões para "quebrar o gelo" e iniciar uma conversa informal.

17   UNIT 2: RELACIONAMENTOS
Estado civil; expressões relativas à cerimônia de casamento.

21   UNIT 3: AFAZERES DOMÉSTICOS
Os diferentes afazeres domésticos; aparelhos domésticos.

25   UNIT: 4: TRÂNSITO
Falando sobre o trânsito e condução de veículos; condução de veículos.

29   UNIT 5: DANDO UMA CARONA PARA UM AMIGO
Oferecendo e aceitando uma carona; pedindo informações sobre como chegar a um lugar.

33   UNIT 6: AS MOEDAS AMERICANAS
Pedindo algumas moedas para o parquímetro; as moedas americanas; convidando alguém para fazer algo.

37   UNIT 7: NA LANCHONETE
Fazendo o pedido em uma lanchonete; comunicação com a garçonete; comidas e bebidas usuais em uma lanchonete.

41   UNIT 8: PLANEJANDO O FIM DE SEMANA
Fazendo planos; falando sobre o clima; atividades de lazer.

45   UNIT 9: CUMPRINDO PRAZOS E METAS
Cumprindo prazos e metas no trabalho; expressões do mundo corporativo; vocabulário e expressões usuais em uma conversa informal entre dois colegas de trabalho.

49   UNIT 10: VOCÊ JÁ EXPERIMENTOU AÇAÍ?
Oferecendo algo para comer; falando que está com fome.

53   UNIT 11: FALANDO SOBRE AS PROVAS NA ESCOLA
Falando sobre a dificuldade de uma prova na escola; matérias escolares; vocabulário e expressões usuais em uma conversa entre dois estudantes.

57	**UNIT 12: UM NOVO LAR** Mudando-se para uma nova casa; falando sobre como você se sente no novo lar.
61	**UNIT 13: ALTERAÇÕES DE HUMOR** O comportamento das pessoas; personalidades; características físicas.
65	**UNIT 14: UMA FASE DIFÍCIL** Atravessando um momento difícil; dando conselhos.
69	**UNIT 15: A IMPORTÂNCIA DE ESTAR MOTIVADO** Falando sobre novos projetos no trabalho; falando sobre como as pessoas se sentem; fazendo elogios.
73	**UNIT 16: PEDINDO FAVORES** Pedindo dinheiro emprestado a um amigo; vocabulário e expressões usuais relativas a dinheiro em uma conversa informal.
77	**UNIT 17: UMA CONSULTA AO DENTISTA** Falando sobre uma consulta ao dentista; tratamento dentário e higiene bucal.
81	**UNIT 18: HORA DO JANTAR!** Cuidando da preparação do jantar; colocando a mesa; vocabulário e expressões usuais relativas a refeições; conversa informal entre marido e esposa sobre o jantar.
85	**UNIT 19: O FERIADO DE AÇÃO DE GRAÇAS** Falando sobre o que as pessoas gostam de fazer nos feriados; atividades de lazer.
89	**UNIT 20: VOCÊ ESTÁ SE SENTINDO MELHOR AGORA?** Falando sobre como você se sente; descrevendo necessidades; conversa informal a respeito de uma festa.
93	**UNIT 21: INDO ÀS COMPRAS** Fazendo compras; pedindo informações em uma loja ou supermercado.
97	**UNIT 22: NO POSTO DE GASOLINA** Abastecendo o carro no posto; conversando com o atendente na loja de conveniências.
101	**UNIT 23: CHEGA DE BEBIDA POR HOJE!** Conversa informal a respeito das atividades de lazer do dia; vocabulário e expressões usuais relativas a bebidas.
105	**UNIT 24: ESPORTES AQUÁTICOS** Falando sobre esportes aquáticos.

109	**UNIT 25: ALIMENTAÇÃO SAUDÁVEL**
	Falando sobre alimentos e dietas e a importância de se alimentar adequadamente.
113	**UNIT 26: LIGAÇÕES TELEFÔNICAS**
	Fazendo ligações telefônicas; vocabulário e expressões usuais relativas a ligações telefônicas; conversa informal.
117	**UNIT 27: ANIMAIS DE ESTIMAÇÃO**
	Falando sobre animais de estimação.
121	**UNIT 28: NO TEATRO**
	Falando sobre uma peça teatral; saindo para se divertir; vocabulário e expressões usuais relativas a entretenimento e diversão.
125	**UNIT 29: O NOVO GERENTE REGIONAL**
	Um novo funcionário na empresa; o relacionamento entre funcionários e chefe; vocabulário e expressões usuais relativas à rotina de trabalho em uma empresa.
129	**UNIT 30: NOVAS EXPERIÊNCIAS**
	Falando e perguntando sobre o uso e experiência com automóveis; vocabulário e expressões usuais relativas a veículos em uma conversa informal.
133	RESPOSTAS
161	GLOSSÁRIO
172	SOBRE O AUTOR

APRESENTAÇÃO

What to say when...? é um livro prático e objetivo, dirigido a todos que desejam revisar e consolidar o vocabulário, expressões e frases usuais empregadas pelos americanos em diversas situações de comunicação cotidiana. Ao longo das 30 unidades do livro, você terá a oportunidade de praticar a compreensão auditiva, a escrita e melhorar a capacidade de se expressar no idioma inglês. O conteúdo cuidadosamente selecionado de **What to say when...?**, em conjunto com o áudio CD gravado por falantes americanos que acompanha o livro, o tornam uma excelente ferramenta para qualquer pessoa que deseje reativar o seu conhecimento do idioma de uma maneira prática e dinâmica, e preparar-se para situações realistas de conversação.

Veja abaixo as seções presentes nas 30 unidades do livro:

DIALOGUE

Cada unidade do livro é iniciada por um diálogo que traz uma situação realista cotidiana. Ao todo **What to say when...?** apresenta 30 diálogos sobre temas variados que garantem a presença de vocabulário e expressões relativas a diversos assuntos. As situações abordadas nos diálogos incluem:

→ Relacionamentos
→ Atividades de lazer
→ Falando sobre prazos e metas no trabalho
→ Pedindo favores
→ Abastecendo o carro no posto de gasolina
→ Fazendo o pedido em uma lanchonete
→ Conduzindo veículos e trânsito
→ Fazendo ligações telefônicas
→ Conversa informal entre amigos
→ Indo às compras
→ Expressando opinião
→ Fazendo elogios
→ Convidando alguém para fazer algo
→ As moedas americanas
→ Os afazeres domésticos
→ Falando sobre animais de estimação
→ Dando uma carona para um amigo
→ Atravessando momentos difíceis

→ Novas experiências
→ Conversando sobre os benefícios de uma alimentação saudável

DIALOGUE COMPREHENSION

Oportunidade de checar a compreensão do diálogo através da atividade *True or False?* contida nesta seção. Você poderá também conferir as respostas desta atividade ao final do livro.

VOCABULARY & EXPRESSIONS

Esta seção traz definições e sinônimos em inglês de palavras e expressões importantes no diálogo. A apresentação desta seção é feita propositalmente apenas em inglês para que você possa ampliar ainda mais o vocabulário. Em caso de dúvida ou dificuldade de compreensão de algum termo apresentado você poderá consultar o glossário inglês-português ao final do livro.

USUAL PHRASES AND QUESTIONS

Você poderá conferir aqui uma seleção de perguntas e frases-chave usuais na conversação cotidiana dos americanos. Esta seção reúne as frases recorrentes e características dos temas abordados em cada unidade, que você poderá também ouvir no CD, revisando o conteúdo de uma forma lúdica e dinâmica e melhorando assim a compreensão auditiva.

EXERCISES

Esta seção oferece a oportunidade de colocar em prática o vocabulário, expressões e frases usuais apresentadas nas seções anteriores. Uma ótima forma de consolidar o rico conteúdo linguístico abordado ao longo das 30 unidades do livro. A seção de exercícios é divida em três tipos de atividades, explicadas abaixo:

I – Fill in the blanks below with a word or expression from the *Vocabulary & Expressions* section. Make sure you use the appropriate verb tense.

São apresentadas cinco sentenças que devem ser completadas com o vocabulário e expressões da seção *Vocabulary & Expressions*. Além de aplicar o vocabulário e expressões corretamente, de tal forma que as frases façam sentido, você deverá também atentar ao uso do tempo verbal apropriado para cada sentença. Um exercício interessante em que a diversidade das sentenças contextualizadas ajuda a consolidar o uso correto do conteúdo apresentado.

II – Write the questions you listen to and then choose the right answer.

Uma atividade que visa desenvolver não somente a habilidade da compreensão auditiva, mas também da escrita, já que você deverá escrever cinco perguntas a partir da audição do CD. Além disso, é também um exercício de múltipla escolha que trabalha o vocabulário e expressões apresentadas anteriormente.

III – Look at the answers and ask questions using the cues provided between parentheses.

Este exercício requer a elaboração de perguntas a partir das respostas e dicas apresentadas entre parênteses. Uma atividade que oferece uma prática importante do uso apropriado dos verbos auxiliares, envolvendo a estrutura gramatical do idioma, bem como o vocabulário. Uma ótima forma de se preparar para fazer perguntas em variadas situações usuais de conversação.

O conjunto de todas as seções de **What to say when...?** oferecem uma forma dinâmica e eficiente de praticar e ativar a fluência no idioma, consolidando assim um importante conteúdo linguístico que o tornará mais confiante e apto à comunicação no idioma inglês. *Enjoy!*

José Roberto A. Igreja

UNIT 1
APRESENTAÇÕES

1

DIALOGUE 1
I'VE HEARD A LOT ABOUT YOU!

Howard: Gary, this is my friend Pamella
Gary: So, you're the famous Pamella, it's nice to finally meet you. I've heard a lot about you!
Pamella: Only good things I hope!
Gary: Sure! (smiling) Howard told me you've just moved in from Seattle. Are you enjoying Miami?
Pamella: I'm loving it! The beaches are gorgeous. This city is a lot of fun.
Gary: I'm glad you're having such a good time here. Let me know if you need any help with anything. I was born and bred here so I know the city like the back of my hand.
Pamella: Thanks Gary!

DIALOGUE COMPREHENSION 1

1. Gary and Pamella have just been introduced to each other.
   True ☐   False ☐
2. Pamella has been living in Miami for a long time.
   True ☐   False ☐
3. Gary had heard about Pamella before.
   True ☐   False ☐
4. Howard is Gary and Pamella's common friend.
   True ☐   False ☐
5. Gary is not very familiar with Miami.
   True ☐   False ☐

VOCABULARY & EXPRESSIONS 1

Gorgeous = very beautiful
Fun = enjoyable
Born and bred = born and raised
Know something like the back of one's hand = know something very well
Let me know = tell me
Have a good time = enjoy oneself

2

USUAL PHRASES AND QUESTIONS 1

I'd like to introduce my friend...
Have you met Andy yet?
I don't think you've met Carol, come on I'll introduce her to you...
Come on, I'll introduce you to a friend of mine...
Nice to meet you!/ Nice to meet you too!
Have we met before?
Were you born here?
You're not from around here, are you?
What do you do for a living?
Do you have a big family?

EXERCISES 1

I – Fill in the blanks below with a word or expression from the *Vocabulary & Expressions* section. Make sure you use the appropriate verb tense.

1. Samantha was _____ in Houston. She's never lived anywhere else.
2. "We had a lot of _____ at the party last night. There was a band
   playing live music," said Mike to a friend.
3. "Why don't you ask Fred how to get there? He _____ this neighborhood _____.
4. "Wow! Look at that blond girl over there. Isn't she _____?" Dave told Brian.
5. _____ if you need any help with those math exercises. I've already solved them," said Gregory to a classmate.

3

II – Write the questions you listen to and then choose the right answer.

1. _____?
a. Yes, I've met them before.
b. Sure, I can introduce her to you.
c. Maybe. You look familiar.
d. Sure, I love meeting new people.

2. _____?
a. No, never. Where is it?
b. That's a beautiful name. I like it.
c. No, not yet. Can you introduce her to me?
d. Yes, I've already been there before.

3. _____?
a. Maybe, let's see what happens.
b. My sister? She loves living in Denver.
c. He moved here when he was five.
d. Not really. I grew up in Denver, but I was actually born in Detroit.

4. _____?
a. Sure, what's her name?
b. I don't have any sisters, just a brother.
c. Sure, what's his name?
d. I didn't know you had any brothers.

5. _____?
a. Yes, I've met Bill before.
b. It's nice to meet you Sheila!
c. Nice meeting you Bill!
d. I'd surely like to meet her.

III – Look at the answers and ask questions using the cues provided between parentheses.

1. (born/ in Boston)
You: _____?
Rachel: No, I was born in South Carolina actually.

2. (meet Sophie/ yet)
You: _____?
Jake: No, not yet. Can you introduce her to me?

3. (like living/ in Los Angeles)
You: _____?
Sally: I love it! L.A. is a great place to live.

4. (my friend/ Norma)
You: _____?
Bill: Nice to meet you Norma!

5. (do/ for a living)
You: _____?
Liz: Me? I'm a vet.

UNIT 2
RELACIONAMENTOS

4 🎧
DIALOGUE 2
FINALLY TYING THE KNOT!
Dave: So, you're finally tying the knot with Kate?
Mick: That's right! We're getting married in September.
Dave: And how long have you been engaged?
Mick: About three years and a half.
Dave: Wow, time does fly! You know, I've been married to Celine for almost ten years now and I sometimes can't believe it!
Mick: Yeah, I know, it's crazy, isn't it? Listen, how would you like to be one of my best men?
Dave: Seriously? That would be an honor Mick! Thanks!

DIALOGUE COMPREHENSION 2
1. Mick and Dave are both single.
   True ☐ False ☐
2. Dave likes the idea of being one of Mick's best men at his wedding.
   True ☐ False ☐
3. Mick has been engaged for over five years.
   True ☐ False ☐
4. Dave is surprised that he's been married for almost ten years.
   True ☐ False ☐
5. Both Kate and Celine are married.
   True ☐ False ☐

VOCABULARY & EXPRESSIONS 2

Tie the knot = get married
Love at first sight = an immediate strong attraction for someone you have just met
Honeymoon = holiday taken by a newly married couple
Newlyweds = a newly married couple
Wedding = marriage ceremony and celebration
Bride = woman just married or about to be married
Groom = man just married or about to be married
Best man = chief male attendant at a wedding
Cheat on = be unfaithful to one's partner in a relationship
Fall in love = begin to experience feelings of love towards
Break up = end a relationship; split up

5

USUAL PHRASES AND QUESTIONS 2

Are you seeing anyone?
Did you know Amy is dating Mike?
How long have you been married/ engaged/ divorced?
I heard Bill and Cindy broke up.
We're getting married next year.
What's your marital status?
Do you know why Fred and Liz broke up/ got divorced?
Dave's girlfriend dumped him, that's why he's so miserable.
I've been dating Carol for almost two years now.
What's your boyfriend/ girlfriend like?

EXERCISES 2

I – Fill in the blanks below with a word or expression from the *Vocabulary & Expressions* section. Make sure you use the appropriate verb tense.

1. Sandy broke up with Ryan because she found out he was _____ her.
2. Franklin _____ with Melissa as soon as he met her. It was _____.
3. Greg has been dating Susan for about four years but he thinks he's not ready to _____ just yet.

4. The _____ are going to Paris on their _____ .
5. Nobody expected Jake and Liz to _____ and call off the _____ .

6 🎧

II – Write the questions you listen to and then choose the right answer.

1. _____?
a. Yes, she did. She broke up with Josh.
b. I do. They're traveling to Europe next month.
c. I heard she found out Josh was cheating on her.
d. No, I don't think Monica would do that.

2. _____?
a. I didn't know he was single.
b. He used to be. He got divorced last year.
c. Yes, he's still single.
d. Yeah, the wedding was great.

3. _____?
a. He'll probably stay single.
b. Not now. Maybe later.
c. I'll talk to him tomorrow.
d. For about two years, I think.

4. _____?
a. In Italy, that's what I heard.
b. Yeah, they were very happy indeed.
c. They love going to the beach.
d. They used to live in Miami, but I heard they moved away.

5. _____?
a. Linda looks great. She's pretty cute as a matter of fact.
b. They should probably get married soon.
c. Not anymore. They broke up a few months ago.
d. I used to, but I haven't seen her in a long time.

III – Look at the answers and ask questions using the cues provided between parentheses.

1. (break up)
You: _____?
Nancy: Well, I found out Terry was seeing someone else. That's why!

2. (married/ how long?)
You: _____?
Ralph: For about five years now.

3. (newlyweds/ honeymoon)
You: _____?
Fred: I heard they are going to Hawaii for their honeymoon.

4. (still/ dating)
You: _____?
Priscilla: Yes, she is. Dana has been dating George for about a year now.

5. (boyfriend/ like)
You: _____?
Sharon: He's kind of shy, but he's very nice.

UNIT 3
AFAZERES DOMÉSTICOS

7

DIALOGUE 3
DO YOU HAVE ANY FAVORITE HOUSEHOLD CHORES?

Ben: So, what kind of chores do you usually do around the house?
Roger: I often do the dishes and I always take the trash out every night, but honestly, I don't do much. My wife has a part-time job so she's the one who does most everything.
Ben: I see. Have you ever had a maid?
Roger: We did once, but only for a short time when Linda was pregnant with Sandy. How about you? Do you have any favorite household chores?
Ben: Well, you know, I can't really choose since I live on my own. I do enjoy ironing my shirts though and taking care of everything else has never been a problem for me really.
Roger: Do you vacuum your apartment very often?
Ben: Once a week on weekends. That's enough to keep it clean!

DIALOGUE COMPREHENSION 3

1. Roger helps his wife with the housework.
   True ☐   False ☐
2. Ben enjoys doing the dishes every day.
   True ☐   False ☐
3. Roger's wife does most of the housework.
   True ☐   False ☐
4. Ben shares an apartment with some more people.
   True ☐   False ☐
5. Doing the housework for Ben is no big deal.
   True ☐   False ☐

VOCABULARY & EXPRESSIONS 3

Household chores = housework such as cleaning, sweeping, doing the dishes etc.
Do the dishes = wash the dishes
Iron = press and smooth with a heated flatiron
Vacuum = clean with a vacuum cleaner
Maid = a woman who works in someone's home doing the housework
Sweep the floor = clean the floor with a broom
On one's own = alone
Mop = clean or wipe with a mop
Washing machine = a machine that washes clothes
Dryer = a machine that dries clothes
Dishwasher = a machine that washes dishes
Oven = a kitchen appliance used for baking or roasting food
Fridge = refrigerator
Stove = a kitchen appliance used for cooking food

8

USUAL PHRASES AND QUESTIONS 3

Can you take the trash out please?
Do you iron your shirts yourself?
I enjoy doing the dishes myself. I don't have a dishwasher.
Do you help your wife with the housework?
How often do you clean your apartment?
The kitchen floor seems to be dirty. Let's wipe it!
What's your favorite household chore?
Can you heat the pizza in the microwave oven for me please?
There's beer in the fridge. Help yourself!
You see those black stains? I think we need to mop the floor.
Do you have a maid?

EXERCISES 3

I – Fill in the blanks below with a word or expression from the *Vocabulary & Expressions* section. Make sure you use the appropriate verb tense.

1. "We need to _____ the apartment at least once a week because of the dust."

2. "I live with my sister, so we share the _____.
   I usually clean the house, sweep and mop the floor and my sister does the dishes," said Rhonda to a friend.
3. "Can you smell it? Rita's baking a cake in the _____," Jennifer told Lucy.
4. "Nobody helps me with the housework. I do it all _____
   my _____," said Martha to a friend.
5. "Is there any butter left in the _____?" Tim asked his roommate.

9

II – Write the questions you listen to and then choose the right answer.

1. _____?
a. Are you kidding? I don't have time for housework!
b. Sure, household chores are part of Jim's daily routine.
c. I enjoy going out on weekends.
d. I love pasta. That's my favorite dish.

2. _____?
a. Sure, I'll get the vacuum cleaner.
b. Sure, I'll do that right now.
c. I can iron my clothes pretty well now.
d. It's in the fridge, I'll get it for you.

3. _____?
a. I used to have a maid, but I don't anymore.
b. Ironing a shirt is not that difficult once you get the hang of it.
c. I'd rather wear a white shirt today.
d. No, I don't have time for that.

4. _____?
a. We took turns driving from L.A. to Las Vegas.
b. I love doing housework.
c. I took it the last time, so it's your turn now!
d. I don't care, just mop the kitchen floor please, it's very dirty.

5. _____?
a. Not as often as we should. We're both very busy, you know.
b. We should definitely hire a maid.
c. Doing the dishes is my favorite household chore.
d. I can take the trash out, don't worry!

III – Look at the answers and ask questions using the cues provided between parentheses.

1. (have/ a maid)
You: _____?
Leyla: No, we don't. We live in a small apartment, so we don't really need one.

2. (favorite/ household chore)
You: _____?
Alan: My favorite household chore? Well, I love ironing my shirts on Saturday morning.

3. (often/ clean/ apartment)
You: _____?
Nina: Once a week, on my day-off.

4. (like/ do/ housework)
You: _____?
Nick: Doing housework? I don't really like it, but I have to.

5. (help me/ housework)
You: _____?
Mike: Sure! What do you want me to do?

UNIT 4
TRÂNSITO

10
DIALOGUE 4
THIS IS A TOW-AWAY ZONE!

Jake: Hey, I wouldn't park here if I were you. You see that sign over there? This is a tow-away zone!
Fred: Thanks Jake, I hadn't noticed it. I'll try and find another parking spot.
Jake: Yeah, you'd better. You sure don't want to get a ticket.
Fred: Ok, let's try the next block. There must be parking spaces there.
Jake: Sure!

DIALOGUE COMPREHENSION 4

1. Jake is the one who is driving.
   True ☐   False ☐
2. Fred has just found a good parking spot.
   True ☐   False ☐
3. Jake and Fred decide to go home since they can't find a parking space.
   True ☐   False ☐
4. Fred thinks they'd better leave the car in a parking lot.
   True ☐   False ☐
5. Fred thinks they can probably find a parking space on the next block.
   True ☐   False ☐

VOCABULARY & EXPRESSIONS 4

Tow-away zone = a no-parking area from which parked cars may be towed away
Parking spot = parking space
Ticket = a traffic fine
Rush hour = a period of heavy traffic when most people are commuting to and from work
Crosswalk = a painted path in a street where traffic must stop to allow pedestrians to get across
Driver's license = an official document allowing someone to drive a car
Traffic jam = a line of vehicles close together, unable to move or moving very slowly because of heavy traffic
Parking meter = a coin-operated device that registers the amount of time purchased for parking a car
Toll plaza = an area where tollbooths are located on a toll road

11

USUAL PHRASES AND QUESTIONS 4

What's the speed limit on this road?
How can I get to main street from here?
This is a two-way street.
You can't park there. Look, there's a tow-away sign over there.
Traffic is always heavy like this during the rush hour.
Do you have some quarters for the parking meter?
How long is your commute to work?
Can you give me directions to the mall from here?
How long does it take you to get to work by car in the morning?
We have to take exit 28 to go to the mall.
Do you know any short-cuts from here?
Is this a toll road?
Slow down, there are some bumps ahead!

EXERCISES 4

I – Fill in the blanks below with a word or expression from the *Vocabulary & Expressions* section. Make sure you use the appropriate verb tense.

1. Make sure you always use the _____ whenever crossing a street.

2. "You'd better slow down. You can get a _____ for going over the speed limit here," Tony advised Nick.
3. We were late to school because of the _____ on main street this morning.
4. "I need some quarters for the _____ Do you have any?" Seth asked Hank.
5. "You cannot park here. This is a _____ Look at the sign over there," said Jeff to a friend.

12

II – Write the questions you listen to and then choose the right answer.

1. _____?
a. Sure, you can get there by car.
b. I'd rather go by bus or subway.
c. Take exit 53 and make a left. You can't miss it.
d. This is a two-way street, so be careful!

2. _____?
a. Sure, I'd love to go shopping today.
b. I prefer going to the mall on weekdays.
c. We have three malls in this city, so you can take your pick.
d. Sure, I'll show you on the map.

3. _____?
a. I got distracted and went over the speed limit.
b. He was arrested for drunk driving.
c. I think he'd left his driver's license at home.
d. The cops? Oh, they were really friendly.

4. _____?
a. I did. I gave them to Lucy.
b. I do. How many do you need?
c. That parking meter was out of order.
d. There's a great parking spot over there.

5. _____?
a. Sure, I always avoid going over the speed limit.
b. I guess it's fifty-five miles, but I'm not sure.
c. Fifty bucks? That's kind of expensive!
d. It'll take about half an hour to get there.

III – Look at the answers and ask questions using the cues provided between parentheses.

1. (How long/ get to school)
You: _____?
Rick: It usually takes me about twenty minutes if the traffic is good.

2. (we/ park here)
You: _____?
Brenda: I don't think so. Look, there's a tow-away zone sign over there.

3. (traffic/ always heavy)
You: _____?
Phil: It's rush hour now, remember?

4. (police/ stop Frank)
You: _____?
Priscilla: I think he was driving way too fast.

5. (quarters/ parking meter)
You: _____?
Randy: No, sorry. I have no coins on me, but I think I can change a five-dollar bill in one of the stores over there.

UNIT 5
DANDO UMA CARONA PARA UM AMIGO

13
DIALOGUE 5
WHERE ARE YOU HEADED?

Tyler: (sound of car horn) Hey Jake! Where are you headed?
Jake: Hi Tyler! Small world! I'm catching a bus to Market Street.
Tyler: Hop in! I'm going that way too.
Jake: Really? Great, I could use a ride.
(sound of car door closing)
Jake: Thanks Tyler!
Tyler: You're welcome!
Jake: So, how's Celine doing?
Tyler: Very good. She got a part-time job recently and she's excited about it.
Jake: Good for her. So, you're helping out more with the household chores, right?
Tyler: Sure, I've always enjoyed doing some work around the house.
Jake: That's good. And how old is Brian now?
Tyler: He turned fifteen last month.
Jake: Fifteen already? Wow! How time flies! Does he have a girlfriend?
Tyler: (smiling) If he does he hasn't told us yet.

DIALOGUE COMPREHENSION 5

1. Tyler doesn't like doing housework.
   True ☐ False ☐
2. Celine is happy about her new job.
   True ☐ False ☐
3. Jake was going to Market Street on foot when he saw Tyler.
   True ☐ False ☐
4. Tyler has a teenage son.
   True ☐ False ☐
5. Jake gives Tyler a ride.
   True ☐ False ☐

VOCABULARY & EXPRESSIONS 5

Be headed = be going to
Hop in = get in
Could use a ride = a ride would be good
Help out = help
Household chores = housework such as cleaning, sweeping, doing the dishes etc.
Turn = become a particular age
How time flies! = time passes very quickly
A ride = a free trip in someone's car
Honk = make a loud noise using the horn of a car

14

USUAL PHRASES AND QUESTIONS 5

Can you give me a ride downtown?
Do you know how to get there?
How can I get to the airport from here?
I'll show you on the map
Is it too far to walk?
How far is it?
Can I get there by subway?
Is it within walking distance?
How many blocks from here?
Where's the nearest bus stop?
Thanks for the ride!

EXERCISES 5

I – Fill in the blanks below with a word or expression from the *Vocabulary & Expressions* section. Make sure you use the appropriate verb tense.

1. "I'm going downtown too. Would you like a _____?" Seth offered Tim.
2. "Stop _____ ! You're going to wake up the neighbors," Rhonda told her husband in the car.
3. "I have lots of things to do in the office today. I wish someone could ____ _____ me _____." said Sarah to a coworker.
4. "My daughter is seventeen now. She'll _____ eighteen on June, 2nd," said Howard to a friend.
5. "If you want a ride just hop in. I'm _____ that way too," Mike told Rick.

15

II – Write the questions you listen to and then choose the right answer.

1. _____?
a. Sure, I can give you a ride.
b. That'd be great, thanks!
c. How about a ride?
d. Yeah, let's give them a ride downtown.

2. _____?
a. Sure, I need to buy some milk.
b. If I were you I'd go there on foot.
c. Yeah, there's one nearby. I'll show you on the map.
d. I've been to a drugstore today.

3. _____?
a. Not really, but I have a GPS.
b. Sure, I'd love to go to the park with you today.
c. I often go jogging in that park.
d. Do you? Great, let's go!

31

4. _____?
a. That's a very busy airport.
b. It takes about forty minutes to get to the airport from here.
c. I wish I could give you a ride.
d. I don't really know, but if I were you I'd take a cab.

5. _____?
a. That's not the mall I told you about.
b. Oh yeah. It's very close.
c. I bought it at the mall last night.
d. I usually go for a walk in the evening.

III – Look at the answers and ask questions using the cues provided between parentheses.

1. (far/ airport)
You: _____?
Kate: About twenty-five miles from here.

2. (get there/ subway)
You: _____?
Dave: Sure, it's very easy to get there by subway.

3. (mall/ near here)
You: _____?
Heather: I have no idea. I'm out of town myself.

4. (tell me/ to get to the train station)
You: _____?
Katrina: Sure, I'll show you on the map.

5. (far/ the park from here)
You: _____?
Mick: About five blocks from here.

UNIT 6
AS MOEDAS AMERICANAS

16
DIALOGUE 6
DO YOU HAVE ANY CHANGE?
Tony: Do you have some quarters?
Chuck: I think I do, what do you need them for?
Tony: For the parking meter. I just parked outside and I have no coins.
Chuck: OK, I think I have some change in my wallet, let me see. Humm, here you go, three quarters.
Tony: Thanks Chuck, that'll do. I'll pay you back tomorrow.
Chuck: Forget about it! Hey, do you wanna have some coffee or something? I feel like having a cappuccino. Maybe we could go to the coffee shop on the corner.
Tony: Great idea, and I can use my credit card there, so it's my treat!

DIALOGUE COMPREHENSION 6
1. Tony needs some coins to buy a cappuccino.
   True ☐   False ☐
2. Chuck has some quarters in his wallet.
   True ☐   False ☐
3. Tony has just parked outside.
   True ☐   False ☐
4. Chuck invites Tony for lunch.
   True ☐   False ☐
5. Tony will pay cash for their drinks.
   True ☐   False ☐

VOCABULARY & EXPRESSIONS 6

Quarter = a coin worth twenty-five cents
Dime = a coin worth ten cents
Nickel = a coin worth five cents
Penny = a coin worth one cent
Parking meter = a coin-operated device that registers the amount of time purchased for parking a car
That'll do = that's enough
Wanna = want to
(It's) my treat! = I'll pay

17

USUAL PHRASES AND QUESTIONS 6

Do you feel like going out tonight?
I'd rather stay home tonight. I'm really tired.
How about lunch tomorrow?
I'm sorry. I'm already busy at lunch time tomorrow. Can I take a rain check?
Do you want to grab a bite to eat at Joe's diner?
How about a drink after work today?
Would you like to see a movie?
How about going to the movies this weekend?
I don't feel like going to the mall today.
Would you rather go out or stay home tonight?
What do you feel like doing tonight?
What would you rather do today?

EXERCISES 6

I – Fill in the blanks below with a word or expression from the *Vocabulary & Expressions* section. Make sure you use the appropriate verb tense.

1. "So, what do you _____ do tonight? Do you feel like going out?" Richard asked Karen.
2. "I have some quarters, nickels and pennies in my pocket, but I don't have any _____," said Josh to a friend who asked him for ten cents.
3. "I have to go outside for a minute. I forgot to put some coins in the _____ . I'll be right back," Dick told his friends.

4. "Let's have dinner at the new Italian restaurant on main street. _____ ! " Bob invited Gary.
5. Andy: "Do you have any coins for the parking meter?"
   Bart: "Let me check my pocket. Humm, I only have two quarters and three dimes."
   Andy: "Good, _____."

18

II − Write the questions you listen to and then choose the right answer.

1. _____?
a. Sure, we could do that.
b. Did you? I had no idea.
c. I'm kind of tired, so I'd rather stay home and relax.
d. I wonder what she's doing tonight.

2. _____?
a. Yep, I've already been to Venice beach!
b. I wish I could go camping, but I don't have a tent.
c. Yeah, we've been to that beach before.
d. Great idea. Maybe we could invite Jeff to come with us.

3. _____?
a. He told me he's not a heavy drinker.
b. I drink about three cups of coffee every day.
c. I'm sorry, I can't tonight.
d. Sure, we went to a pub last night. It was a lot of fun.

4. _____?
a. I'd love that. I'm kind of hungry. Let's go!
b. No, I don't have a clue who Ruby is.
c. I love my mom's food. She's a great cook.
d. Dinner? Oh no, not tonight. Maybe some other time.

5. _____?
a. No, I've never been there.
b. I need to go shopping for sneakers. I think I'll go to the mall.
c. I'd do that if I had time.
d. Sure, let's do it together.

III – Look at the answers and ask questions using the cues provided between parentheses.

1. (want/ go out)
You: _____?
Rita: Not really. I'd rather stay home and watch a movie.

2. (lunch/ tomorrow)
You: _____?
Linda: I'm sorry, I can't tomorrow. Can I take a rain check?

3. (coins/ parking meter)
You: _____?
Joe: Yeah, I have some quarters in my pocket.

4. (rather do/ tonight)
You: _____?
Stephanie: Maybe we could go see a play.

5. (enjoy/ show last night)
You: _____?
Jake: I did. It was great. I had a lot of fun.

UNIT 7

NA LANCHONETE

19

DIALOGUE 7
WHAT DOES THE DELUXE BURGER COME WITH?

Waitress: Hi, I'm Amy. I'll be your waitress tonight. Are you ready to order or do you need some time to think it over?
Jake: Hi Amy, I think I can order now. I'm actually curious about your deluxe burger. What does it come with?
Waitress: That's a big sandwich sir, it's got two burgers, mayo, lettuce, tomatoes, relish and fries on the side.
Jake: Wow, sounds good to me. I'm famished, so I'll have one of those.
Waitress: Good, how about your sir?
Ryan: Make it two.
Waitress: Ok, very good. Anything to drink?
Jake: A regular coke for me please.
Ryan: Do you have freshly squeezed orange juice?
Waitress: We do. Would you like one of those?
Ryan: Yes, please.
Waitress: Sure sir, I'll be right back with your drinks.
Jake: Thanks!

DIALOGUE COMPREHENSION 7

1. Jake and Ryan are not ready to order yet.
    True ☐   False ☐
2. Ryan orders the same thing as Jake.
    True ☐   False ☐
3. The deluxe burger comes with just one burger.
    True ☐   False ☐

4. Jake is very hungry.
   True ☐ False ☐
5. The waitress was rude to them.
   True ☐ False ☐

VOCABULARY & EXPRESSIONS 7
Order = ask for food or drink in a restaurant
Deluxe = better or superior in quality
Burger = a hamburger
Mayo = mayonnaise
Relish = sauce eaten with food such as hot dogs, hamburgers etc.; condiment
Fries = French fries
Famished = very hungry; starving
Freshly squeezed = that has just been squeezed
Squeeze = press something, such as liquid out of an orange**Put on weight** = gain weight
Go on a diet = try to lose weight by following a specific diet or eating less food
Fast food = food such as hamburgers, pizza and fries that is prepared and served quickly

---

20 🎧
USUAL PHRASES AND QUESTIONS 7
Are you ready to order?
Would you like to order now or do you need some more time?
What can I get you guys?
Can I see the menu please?
How would you like your steak sir?
I'd like my steak rare/ medium/ well-done please.
Can you get me a straw please?
I'll have the spaghetti with meatballs.
Can I get you anything else?
I'll be right back with your drinks.
Can you get me another fork/ spoon/ knife please?
How about dessert?
Can you bring us the check please?

EXERCISES 7

I – Fill in the blanks below with a word or expression from the *Vocabulary & Expressions* section. Make sure you use the appropriate verb tense.

1. "I'm _____ . Let's go get something to eat," Dave told Terry.
2. "Hey, you look fatter than the last time I saw you. Have you been _____ ?" George asked Nick.
3. "I'm sick and tired of _____ . Can we have a real meal tonight?" said Fred to Samantha.
4. "Would you like to _____ now sir?" the waitress asked Brian.
5. "I really need to _____ . I'm overweight", Fred told a friend.

21

II – Write the questions you listen to and then choose the right answer.

1. _____?
a. I do like steaks.
b. I love burgers. Don't you?
c. I guess I'll have the vegetable soup first, please.
d. Well-done please!

2. _____?
a. You don't need to say it again. I got you!
b. Let's see, maybe tomorrow.
c. A cheeseburger and fries please.
d. I wish I had time for that.

3. _____?
a. I guess so. What does the grilled chicken come with?
b. Yeah, I'm all set. Let's go.
c. That's not in the menu.
d. Nope, she's not ready yet. We need to wait a little longer.

4. _____?
a. No, I didn't do anything else.
b. No, thanks. Just the check please.
c. Ok, what else do you need?
d. Sure, let's go get something to eat.

5. _____?
a. Dessert? Oh no, not for me, thanks. I'm stuffed.
b. That spoon seems to be dirty.
c. Sure! Just a minute sir, I'll be right back.
d. No problem, I'll get you another fork.

III – Look at the answers and ask questions using the cues provided between parentheses.

1. (get me/ straw please)
You: _____?
Dana A straw? Sure, just a minute sir.

2. (ready/ order)
You: _____?
Fred: Yeah, I think I can order now.

3. (like/ steak ma'am)
You: _____?
Carol: Medium please.

4. (get you/ anything else)
You: _____?
Harry: Just the check please.

5. (about/ dessert)
You: _____?
Bill: No, thanks! I think I'll skip dessert. I'm stuffed.

UNIT 8
PLANEJANDO O FIM DE SEMANA

22
DIALOGUE 8
PLANS FOR THE WEEKEND

Seth: So, what do you feel like doing today honey?
Bianca: I thought maybe we could go bicycle riding at the park.
Seth: Bicycle riding? Humm, I'd like that. The weather seems perfect for bicycle riding today.
Bianca: Yeah, I heard the weatherman on the radio last night. He said it would be sunny the whole weekend.
Seth: That's good news, seems like a great weekend for outdoor activities! How about playing tennis in the afternoon?
Bianca: Maybe we could do that tomorrow. I feel like lying down on the grass and getting a tan later on.
Seth: Sure honey, that would be good. I could definitely do with some sun rays. I sometimes think I look way too white!
Bianca: Yeah, but we should also wear some sunscreen to protect our skin, remember? Listen, I just had an idea. Why don't we fix some sandwiches to take to the park?
Seth: A picnic? Sure, why not? Looks like our Saturday is going to be real different and fun!
Bianca: Yeah, I think it's good to break the routine once in a while.

DIALOGUE COMPREHENSION 8

1. Seth thinks he could benefit from being exposed to the sun.
   True ☐   False ☐

2. Bianca would rather not play tennis today.
   True ☐ False ☐
3. According to the weatherman there will be a storm.
   True ☐ False ☐
4. Bianca thinks wearing sunscreen is not really necessary.
   True ☐ False ☐
5. Both Seth and Bianca think a picnic would be fun.
   True ☐ False ☐

VOCABULARY & EXPRESSIONS 8

Feel like = desire or want to do something
Honey = dear
Go bicycle riding = go for a bike ride
Weatherman = weather forecaster
Outdoor activities = activities in the open air
Lie down = move into a reclining position
Get a tan = get a suntan
Could definitely do with = could certainly benefit from
Sunscreen = cream used to protect the skin from being burned by the sun
Fix some sandwiches = prepare some sandwiches
Fun = enjoyable; amusing
Once in a while = sometimes

23

USUAL PHRASES AND QUESTIONS 8

What do you feel like doing this weekend?
Would you rather stay home or go out tonight?
I feel like swimming.
Why don't we go dancing tonight?
We went fishing last weekend. It was a lot of fun.
Do you like to go camping?
Would you like to go bowling tonight?
Have you ever been to that amusement park?
How about going to the movies tonight?
What's the weather like today?
It's sunny/ cloudy/ rainy/ windy/ snowy
What's the weather forecast for the weekend?
Does it snow in the winter?

It's too cold to go swimming today.
I hate rainy weather.

EXERCISES 8

I – Fill in the blanks below with a word or expression from the *Vocabulary & Expressions* section. Make sure you use the appropriate verb tense.

1. Todd: "Do you _____ going to the beach this weekend?"
   Rachel: "Sure! It would be great to _____ on the sand and _____."
2. "Come on honey, it's time to get up! I'll _____ you some breakfast," Hillary told her husband.
3. "You'd better put on some _____. Those rays could be harmful to your health," Daisy advised her husband.
4. "Did you hear what the _____ just said? It looks like we're in for a storm," said Doug to a friend.
5. "I'm feeling a little dizzy. I think I'm going to _____ for a while," Steph told Nick.

24

II – Write the questions you listen to and then choose the right answer.

1. _____?
a. Maybe. That will depend on what happens later.
b. I think I would prefer to stay home and watch a comedy show.
c. I'd rather not talk about that now.
d. Sure, let's do it!

2. _____?
a. It'll be mostly sunny on Saturday, but it might rain a little on Sunday.
b. Yeah, that's what the weatherman said.
c. I don't really like very hot weather.
d. I prefer mild weather.

3. _____?
a. I wish I could go fishing this weekend.
b. They did. They had a great time there.

c. Bowling? Not really. Maybe some other time.
d. Sure! I love surfing.

4. _____?
a. I went ice skating at the local rink.
b. No, I haven't met them yet.
c. That would be awesome!
d. Oh yeah, the rides there are great.

5. _____?
a. I like summer days.
b. That's my favorite kind of weather.
c. It's colder than yesterday. I think you should put on a jacket before going out.
d. I'm feeling a little cold.

III – Look at the answers and ask questions using the cues provided between parentheses.

1. (like/ go camping)
You: _____?
Nick: I do. I love to go camping. As a matter of fact I've just bought a new tent.

2. (weather forecast/ weekend)
You: _____?
Mary: The weatherman said it will be a little cloudy on Saturday, but the sun might come out on Sunday.

3. (feel like/ go dancing)
You: _____?
Rita: Yeah, I'd love to go dancing tonight. Great idea!

4. (go/ to the movies/ tonight)
You: _____?
Monica: Sorry, I think I'd rather stay home tonight. It's too cold to go out.

5. (rather do/ today)
You: _____?
Leyla: I don't know! Do you have any suggestions?

UNIT 9

CUMPRINDO PRAZOS E METAS

25

DIALOGUE 9
WE MAY NEED TO WORK OVERTIME TO MEET THE DEADLINE.

Richard: How's the new project coming along?
Brian: So far so good, but I'm afraid we may need to work overtime to meet the deadline.
Richard: Really? Why's that?
Brian: Well, we've had some setbacks with the initial planning of the logistics. Besides that two people in our department are on leave now.
Richard: Sorry to hear that! Let me know if there's anything I could do to help you guys out.
Brian: Thanks Richard! We should still be doing OK if we don't hit any more snags, so let's keep our fingers crossed!
Richard: Sure Brian, I'm sure everything will turn out fine in the end.

DIALOGUE COMPREHENSION 9

1. According to Brian they are ahead of schedule with the project.
   True ☐   False ☐
2. Brian's department is short-staffed.
   True ☐   False ☐

3. Richard shows no interest in the current situation of the project.
   True ☐   False ☐
4. Richard offers Brian help with the project.
   True ☐   False ☐
5. Both Richard and Brian believe things will eventually turn out fine.
   True ☐   False ☐

VOCABULARY & EXPRESSIONS 9

Come along = develop; make progress
So far so good = up to this point all is OK
Meet the deadline = have something finished on time
Setback = delay
On leave = absent with permission from work
Hit a snag = run into an unexpected problem or difficulty
Keep one's fingers crossed = wish luck for someone or something
Turn out fine = end well
Short-staffed = without enough workers
Workload = the amount of work that a person has to do

26

USUAL PHRASES AND QUESTIONS 9

What's your company's core business?
Who are the main competitors in your segment?
How many people attended the meeting?
What's your e-mail address please?
There's a great demand for this kind of product right now.
Does your company offer internship programs?
We need to hire two new systems analysts for the IT department.
Why did they call off the meeting?
I'll e-mail the spreadsheet to you later today.
Networking plays a major role in the corporate world.
What's the dress code where you work?
Will your company have a booth at the international trade show this year?
Could you send us some samples of your products?
You're doing a great job. Keep up the good work!

EXERCISES 9

I – Fill in the blanks below with a word or expression from the *Vocabulary & Expressions* section. Make sure you use the appropriate verb tense.

1. "Our _____ has practically doubled in the past few months. We badly need to hire some experienced sales reps," Mike told a coworker.
2. "How many employees are _____ in your department at the moment?" Mr. Dreyfus asked Mark.
3. "Our boss is sure happy the project is _____ fine," said Bill to a coworker.
4. Although they hit a few snags with the project they were still able to keep things under control and _____ .
5. "So, I heard the shipping department is _____ . Hasn't HR found anyone qualified yet?" Dennis asked Joe.

27 🎧

II – Write the questions you listen to and then choose the right answer.

1. _____?
a. No, that's not their new product.
b. I guess so, that is if there are no more setbacks.
c. By mid-September, if everything goes according to schedule.
d. Yes, they will.

2. _____?
a. It's very casual. We can pretty much wear whatever we want to.
b. I don't like to wear a suit and tie every day.
c. I find sneakers very comfortable.
d. It's a great place to work really!

3. _____?
a. I'm not familiar with the details of that project.
b. Sure, there's a great demand for this kind of project.
c. They'll hire some new sales reps soon.
d. Right now we're behind schedule with the project, so we'll need to work overtime to make sure we meet the deadline.

4. _____?
a. That kind of program is feasible.
b. Yeah, we have six interns at the moment.
c. You'd better delegate some tasks to your intern.
d. The internship program proved to be really effective.

5. _____?
a. The meeting is scheduled for next Tuesday at 9:00 am.
b. Sure, I attended that meeting.
c. I heard he had a family emergency.
d. I'll brief you on the highlights of the meeting.

III – Look at the answers and ask questions using the cues provided between parentheses.

1. (people/ attend the meeting)
You: _____?
Thelma: I'm not sure, but I think about twelve people. Some of the sales reps couldn't make it as they were out visiting clients.

2. (e-mail address)
You: _____?
Tom: It's tom.phraser@cyberspace.com

3. (project/ come along)
You: _____?
Michelle: Very good. Everything seems to be running smoothly.

4. (new rule/ apply to everyone in the company)
You: _____?
Jesse: I guess so, but we'll find out more about it in our weekly meeting.

5. (get along with/ coworkers)
You: _____?
Beth: I do. They're all very friendly.

UNIT 10
VOCÊ JÁ EXPERIMENTOU AÇAÍ?

28

DIALOGUE 10
IT DOESN'T JUST TASTE GOOD, IT'S ALSO VERY HEALTHY!

Will: What's that purple-colored thing you're eating?
Teddy: You mean to say you've never had açaí?
Will: To be honest I don't remember ever eating that. Does it taste good?
Teddy: Here, have some. You're gonna love it.
Will: Humm, yeah, it does taste good!
Teddy: It doesn't just taste good, it's also very healthy!
Will: Really? Now, tell me the downside, is it rich in calories?
Teddy: Yeah, a little, but I wouldn't worry about it if I were you. You know, you can prepare it in different ways. Some people like to add granola, banana and even condensed milk to it. I myself like it plain.
Will: I've never seen it around. Can I just buy it anywhere?
Teddy: Well, maybe not just anywhere, but some big supermarket chains are now selling it. It's imported from Brazil.
Will: Sounds good! Thanks for the tip!

DIALOGUE COMPREHENSION 10

1. Will has never had açaí.
    True ☐   False ☐
2. Teddy likes açaí with granola and condensed milk.
    True ☐   False ☐

3. People eat açaí in many different ways.
   True ☐ False ☐
4. Açaí is a typically Brazilian product.
   True ☐ False ☐
5. Will doesn't think açaí tastes good.
   True ☐ False ☐

VOCABULARY & EXPRESSIONS 10

Taste = have a particular flavor
Healthy = good for your health
Downside = negative aspect of something; disadvantage
Plain = with no additional ingredients
Tip = a useful piece of information
Yummy = delicious

29

USUAL PHRASES AND QUESTIONS 10

This cake tastes great!
How about some coffee?
Would you like some ice tea?
Are you hungry?
I'm starving!/ I'm famished!
I feel like having some chocolate.
Let's go grab a bite to eat at Joe's diner.
Have you ever eaten that before?
How does it taste?
Do you like doughnuts and muffins?
What flavor is it?
I'll have a strawberry milk shake.

EXERCISES 10

I – Fill in the blanks below with a word or expression from the *Vocabulary & Expressions* section. Make sure you use the appropriate verb tense.

1. Betty: "Would you like some cream with your coffee?"
   Matt: "No, thanks! I like it _____."
2. One of the _____ of being a celebrity is the lack of privacy.

3. "I wish I could have some more of your _____ strawberry pie, but I'm on a diet," said Gary to Melinda.
4. "That was a very useful piece of information. Thanks for the _____!" Chuck told Larry.
5. "Hummm! This sandwich _____ good. What's in it?"

30

II – Write the questions you listen to and then choose the right answer.

1. _____?
a. Yep, it tastes yummy!
b. No, strawberry is my favorite flavor.
c. Sure, help yourself!
d. That chocolate muffin tastes delicious!

2. _____?
a. I've been to that diner before.
b. Sure, let's go, I'm starving!
c. It does taste good. Thanks!
d. A burger and fries please.

3. _____?
a. That's my favorite flavor.
b. I think I'll have some strawberries. I love fruit.
c. Sure, I love pancakes.
d. Vanilla. Humm, it tastes real good!

4. _____?
a. No, thanks! I'm OK.
b. Yep, they have a new coffee maker.
c. Sure, I'll make some tea.
d. Yeah, it's really hot.

5. _____?
a. That's a big sandwich.
b. I'll fix you a sandwich.
c. No, thanks! Maybe later.
d. I have no idea, but it tastes really good.

III – Look at the answers and ask questions using the cues provided between parentheses.

1. (like/ ice tea)
You: _____?
Karen: Yes, thank you!

2. (you/ hungry)
You: _____?
Tony: Yeah, I'm famished!

3. (like/ go out/ for dinner)
You: _____?
Melissa: No, I'd rather stay home. Maybe we could order a pizza.

4. (cream/ sugar)
You: _____?
Ted: No, thanks. I like my coffee plain.

5. (it/ taste)
You: _____?
Nicholas: It tastes great! What's it made of?

UNIT 11

FALANDO SOBRE AS PROVAS NA ESCOLA

31

DIALOGUE 11
THE TEST WAS A CINCH!

Jeff: How was the chemistry test this morning?
Rod: A cinch! I was really surprised, I didn't expect it to be so easy.
Jeff: Really?
Rod: Yeah, I think everyone will score highly on this one. I'm worried about the other tests though.
Jeff: How many more left?
Rod: Four more tough ones, I'm afraid. I think I may need to pull an all-nighter for the American literature test. I need to read about 300 pages!
Jeff: Wow, good luck Rod!
Rod: Yeah, I guess I could use some luck. Thanks Jeff!

DIALOGUE COMPREHENSION 11

1. Rod thinks the chemistry test was a piece of cake.
   True ☐   False ☐
2. Jeff doesn't seem interested in Rod's tests at school.
   True ☐   False ☐
3. Rod is not worried at all about the tests.
   True ☐   False ☐
4. There are still four easy tests left for Rod to do.
   True ☐   False ☐
5. Jeff wishes Rod luck with his tests.
   True ☐   False ☐

VOCABULARY & EXPRESSIONS 11

A cinch = very easy; a piece of cake
Score highly = get a good score
Tough = hard; difficult
Pull an all-nighter = study all night
Could use some luck = some luck would be good
No brainer = very easy; a piece of cake
Brainy = intelligent; clever
Major = main subject studied by a college student
Assignment = work that you must do as part of a course; task

32

USUAL PHRASES AND QUESTIONS 11

What's your favorite subject at school?
I've always liked biology/ chemistry/ history/ math/ physics/ geography.
   What's your major?
Where did you go to college?
What was your score on that test?
I'll have to cram for the tests next week.
The test was a piece of cake!
Have you done your history assignment yet?
How was the test this morning?
Did you get a good score on the test?

EXERCISES 11

I – Fill in the blanks below with a word or expression from the *Vocabulary & Expressions* section. Make sure you use the appropriate verb tense.

1. Edward is a _____ student. He always _____ on all the tests.
2. "What a _____ test! I left some questions unanswered. Just too difficult," said Roger to a classmate after the test.
3. "What was your _____ in college?" Fred asked Bart.
4. "I'll have to _____ for the test tomorrow," said Brian to a friend.
5. "Have you done your geography _____ yet? We need to hand it in next Tuesday, right?" Jake asked a classmate.

33

II – Write the questions you listen to and then choose the right answer.

1. _____?
a. That's a tough subject.
b. I guess geography is easier than math.
c. Sure, I love studying chemistry.
d. My favorite subject? History, I've always liked history.

2. _____?
a. I hope so! I'll find out tomorrow.
b. I may have to put an all-nighter for the test.
c. What's the score?
d. Nope, he didn't show up yesterday.

3. _____?
a. Yep, the assignment is due tomorrow.
b. She did it all by herself.
c. Yes, I have. I guess I was inspired!
d. I'll probably score highly on this one.

4. _____?
a. Not everyone likes geography, you know.
b. I hate it!
c. He used to be a math teacher, but that was a long time ago.
d. I have two tests tomorrow, that's why I can't go out tonight.

5. _____?
a. That's right. They all did the same test.
b. It was really cold.
c. Funny? How can you say that?
d. A cinch! I think everyone will get a good score on this one.

III – Look at the answers and ask questions using the cues provided between parentheses.

1. (your/ major)
You: _____?
Freddy: Computer science. And yours?

2. (done/ assignment)
You: _____?
Rachel: Not yet. I plan to do it tomorrow afternoon.

3. (go/ high school)
You: _____?
Dennis: I went to Bentley high. I had great teachers there.

4. (test/ difficult)
You: _____?
Dave: No, not difficult at all. It was a piece of cake!

5. (your/ score)
You: _____?
Camila: I don't know. I'll find out tomorrow.

UNIT 12
UM NOVO LAR

34
DIALOGUE 12
DO YOU PLAN ON THROWING A HOUSEWARMING PARTY?

Sharon: The view from your penthouse is fabulous! My congrats! I guess it does make a difference being on the top floor, huh?
Tyler: Yeah, I moved in recently so I'm still not used to it.
Sharon: Do you plan on throwing a housewarming party?
Tyler: I thought about it, but I think I'll need some time to settle in first. I still have lots of boxes I need to open and a lot of stuff to put into place, you know.
Sharon: I could help you out with the boxes. I love organizing things around the house.
Tyler: Do you? Well, I could definitely use some help. Thanks Sharon!
Sharon: You're welcome. Do you wanna start now?
Tyler: Uh, you mean, just now?
Sharon: Yeah, the sooner the better, right?
Tyler: I guess you're right, but let's just have some coffee first. I have my compact espresso machine up and running.
Sharon: Sounds good!

DIALOGUE COMPREHENSION 12

1. Tyler has been living in that apartment for quite some time.
   True ☐   False ☐
2. Sharon has already been invited to Tyler's housewarming party.
   True ☐   False ☐
3. Sharon seems to be a very helpful friend.
   True ☐   False ☐
4. Tyler needs to unpack his espresso machine.
   True ☐   False ☐
5. Sharon probably likes coffee.
   True ☐   False ☐

VOCABULARY & EXPRESSIONS 12

Penthouse = an apartment located at the top of a tall building
My congrats = congratulations
Move in = move into a new house or apartment
Housewarming party = a party given after moving into a new place
Settle in = become familiar and comfortable with a new place, such as a new home
Stuff = things
Up and running = working; functioning
Sounds good! = that's a good idea!

35 🎧

USUAL PHRASES AND QUESTIONS 12

Do you live in a big house?
Have you always lived in an apartment?
Who do you live with?
Do you have a maid?
Would you rather live somewhere else?
How many bedrooms are there?
Is there a balcony?
Do you like living in the suburbs?
I need to buy new furniture...
How much is the rent?
The rent plus the utilities work out to about one thousand dollars.
Do you have good neighbors?

Is the neighborhood safe/ quiet?
Have you ever lived abroad?

EXERCISES 12

I – Fill in the blanks below with a word or expression from the *Vocabulary & Expressions* section. Make sure you use the appropriate verb tense.

1. "We need to get the heater _____ . The winter is coming soon and it will be too cold in here," said Greg to his roommate.
2. Josh: "Do you want to grab a bite to eat at Joe's diner?"
   Trevor: "_____ Let's go!"
3. "You've done a great job. _____ !" Miles told Hank.
4. "Can I leave my _____ here?" Dave asked Fred.
5. "Your new apartment looks great and it's really spacious. Do you plan on giving a _____ ?"

36

II – Write the questions you listen to and then choose the right answer.

1. _____?
a. I used to live in a quiet place.
b. Sure, I agree with you.
c. Oh yeah, very quiet and I like it that way!
d. He told me the neighborhood where he lives is sometimes noisy.

2. _____?
a. Sure, I like living there.
b. It's not so big, but it's all right.
c. I think he has two roommates.
d. I used to live alone, but now my girlfriend has just moved into my apartment.

3. _____?
a. No, not yet, but I plan to spend some time in Europe.
b. I'd love to live there.
c. Yes, I've seen that documentary before.
d. That's cool!

4. _____?
a. That's the size of it?
b. It's quite spacious. There are three bedrooms, a kitchen, a big living room and a balcony.
c. No, not so small.
d. It was quite informative. I really liked that lecture.

5. _____?
a. I have good neighbors, I can't really complain.
b. I'd rather live in a bigger apartment, but I can't afford it now.
c. No, I used to live in a big house in the suburbs when I was a teenager.
d. No, the white house is bigger.

III − Look at the answers and ask questions using the cues provided between parentheses.

1. (how much/ rent)
You: _____?
Sally: It's about nine hundred dollars a month, with the utilities included.

2. (live/ with)
You: _____?
Terry: With my wife and my two daughters.

3. (have/ good neighbors)
You: _____?
Jake: I do. They're very friendly.

4. (apartment/ big)
You: _____?
Mitch: No, it's very small.

5. (how many/ bedrooms)
You: _____?
Celine: Just one bedroom.

UNIT 13
ALTERAÇÕES DE HUMOR

37
DIALOGUE 13
I'M USED TO HIS MOOD SWINGS!

Mick: Have you seen Tyler around?
Karen: Yeah, I think he's in the meeting room, but I wouldn't talk to him now if I were you.
Mick: Why's that?
Karen: He's in a bad mood. Grumpy, if you know what I mean. That's why.
Mick: Really? Well, I need to clear up some doubts about the financial spreadsheet and I can't wait. I'm used to his mood swings anyway. Thanks!
Karen: Ok, I hope he doesn't take his bad mood out on you. Good luck!
Mick: Thanks Karen!

DIALOGUE COMPREHENSION 13

1. Karen has no idea where Tyler is.
   True ☐   False ☐
2. Mick needs to talk to Tyler about the housewarming party.
   True ☐   False ☐
3. Karen advises Mick not to talk to Tyler right now.
   True ☐   False ☐
4. Tyler is feeling great today.
   True ☐   False ☐
5. Mick decides to talk to Tyler later.
   True ☐   False ☐

VOCABULARY & EXPRESSIONS 13

Grumpy = annoyed and dissatisfied; irritable
Clear up = make clear or more easily understood
Spreadsheet = a computer program for financial calculations
Mood swings = extreme or rapid change in mood
Take out on = release bad feelings such as anger, bad mood etc. on someone
Outgoing = friendly; sociable
Reliable = someone or something that can be trusted
Selfish = thinking only about oneself, not caring about other people

38

USUAL PHRASES AND QUESTIONS 13

What does your new boyfriend look like?
He's tall/ short/ average height
He has black/ blonde/ curly hair
He has a beard/ mustache/ goatee
He has green/ blue/ brown eyes
What's your sister like?
She's outgoing and friendly
She's talkative and funny
She's serious and reliable
Do you look like your mom/ dad?
Is he always so boring/ demanding/ arrogant like that?
He's in a good/ bad mood
She's the spitting image of her mother

EXERCISES 13

I – Fill in the blanks below with a word or expression from the *Vocabulary & Expressions* section. Make sure you use the appropriate verb tense.

1. "You have the right to be angry, but it's not my fault we missed the deadline, so don't _____ it _____ me."
2. "You can definitely count on Jeff. He's very _____."
3. "Can you e-mail me the _____ we worked on this morning? I need to check some figures before our meeting with the managers," said Frank to a coworker.

4. "Roger is so _____. He only thinks about himself!" said Brian to a friend.
5. Mike always gets a little _____ when he doesn't have enough sleep.

39

II – Write the questions you listen to and then choose the right answer.

1. _____?
a. Sure, I like her very much.
b. Nobody likes her.
c. She's a great student.
d. She's outgoing and talkative. She has a lot of friends.

2. _____?
a. Yeah, my dad does that all the time.
b. No, not really, she's usually very friendly.
c. I met her a couple of years ago.
d. I don't like rude and arrogant people.

3. _____?
a. I heard he had a heated argument with his girlfriend. That's why he's so grumpy today.
b. I'll do that no matter what.
c. That seems to be the problem.
d. He's very tall and he has curly blonde hair.

4. _____?
a. That's what I keep telling myself.
b. No, I'm taller than she is.
c. Oh no! We don't really look alike.
d. I used to, but I don't any more.

5. _____?
a. That's not my dad. That's my uncle.
b. My dad? He has short black hair and light brown eyes. He's also tall like myself.
c. My dad? He went to the mall to watch a movie.
d. Just like my mom's hair.

III – Look at the answers and ask questions using the cues provided between parentheses.

1. (Bob/ look like)
You: _____?
Peggy: He has blonde hair and blue eyes. He's very handsome!

2. (matter/ with Dave)
You: _____?
Jake: He has a headache. That's why he's in such a bad mood today.

3. (Paul/ always so arrogant like this)
You: _____?
Tim: Yes, he is. Nobody here likes him.

4. (is/ boss like)
You: _____?
Norma: He's very demanding, but he's also very supportive. I can't complain really.

5. (look like/ mom or dad)
You: _____?
Brooke: I look just like my mom. People say I'm the spitting image of my mother!

UNIT 14
UMA FASE DIFÍCIL

40

DIALOGUE 14
MAYBE HE SHOULD TAKE A FEW DAYS OFF AND UNWIND.

Jesse: What was that all about?
Ruth: You mean the screaming? Oh, don't worry! That was just Brian. He's in a terrible mood today.
Jesse: Is he? Gee! I mean, this is not a good place for making a scene.
Ruth: You're right, you know he's going through a tough time.
Jesse: I can understand that. I guess we all have problems in our private lives. Perhaps he should see a shrink or do something about it.
Ruth: You know what? Maybe he should take a few days off and unwind. It would do him good.
Jesse: I couldn't agree with you more. Ok, I'll talk to him about it.

DIALOGUE COMPREHENSION 14

1. Ruth doesn't have a clue what's going on.
   True ☐   False ☐
2. Jesse thinks Brian should do something about it.
   True ☐   False ☐
3. Ruth tells Jesse that she's been seeing a shrink.
   True ☐   False ☐
4. Jesse agrees with Ruth that taking a few days off would do Brian good.
   True ☐   False ☐
5. Jesse asks Ruth to talk to Brian about it.
   True ☐   False ☐

VOCABULARY & EXPRESSIONS 14

Scream = shout
Make a scene = be loud and rude
Gee! = a general exclamation of surprise or enthusiasm
Tough = hard; difficult
Shrink = psychiatrist; psychoanalyst
Take a few days off = have a few days free from work
Unwind = relax

41
USUAL PHRASES AND QUESTIONS 14

What would you do if you were in my shoes?
If I were you I wouldn't do that
Can you give me some advice on...
Why don't you try to talk to her again?
Perhaps you should take a few days off and relax
What do you think I should do?
Can't you try to work things out with him?
What would you advise me to do?

EXERCISES 14

I – Fill in the blanks below with a word or expression from the *Vocabulary & Expressions* section. Make sure you use the appropriate verb tense.

1. "The last question on the test was a _____ . one. Did you answer it at all?" Jake asked a classmate.
2. "In my opinion he needs professional help. Has he considered seeing a _____?" Jeff asked Brooke.
3. "I think I heard someone _____ outside. Let me check what's going on," said Hank to his wife.
4. "Stop _____ . Everyone is looking at us!" Howard told Norma in the restaurant.
5. "You look really tired. Why don't you _____ and relax?" Doug told a coworker.

42

II – Write the questions you listen to and then choose the right answer.

1. _____?
a. Those shoes don't fit me.
b. I've just bought a new pair of shoes.
c. I'd tell her the truth.
d. I'd rather stay home and watch the comedy show.

2. _____?
a. Sure, what do you need?
b. Sure, that's what I need.
c. Sure, I could certainly ask them to.
d. Maybe, but I need to check with him first.

3. _____?
a. No, she doesn't work every day.
b. I don't think so. She's mad at me like she's never been before.
c. I work out at the gym four times a week.
d. No, I don't think she works out regularly. She's too busy for that.

4. _____?
a. I take off my shoes as soon as I get home.
b. I usually take a nap after lunch. Don't you?
c. It was too hot in there, so I took off my jacket.
d. I can't do that now. I have a deadline to meet.

5. _____?
a. You always do that, don't you?
b. Did she really do that?
c. Perhaps you should try to talk to them again.
d. Maybe, let's see what happens.

III – Look at the answers and ask questions using the cues provided between parentheses.

1. (you/ do/ if/ in my shoes)
You: _____?
Hank: I'd probably tell them the whole truth.

2. (try/ talk to her/ again)
You: _____?
George: I've tried to do that, but she won't listen to me.

3. (advise me/ do)
You: _____?
Roy: I don't really know. It seems like a pretty difficult situation.

4. (ask/ you something)
You: _____?
Bart: Sure! I'm all ears.

5. (think/ I should do)
You: _____?
Ralph: Maybe you could try to explain the situation to them again.

UNIT 15

A IMPORTÂNCIA DE ESTAR MOTIVADO

43

DIALOGUE 15
MOTIVATION IS EVERYTHING.

Damon: I heard you finally got to talk to Hank. So, how was it?
Barbara: Great! We had an enlightening conversation.
Damon: Really?
Barbara: Yep! He's so gung ho about the new project. I mean, it's contagious. I left his office feeling very enthusiastic.
Damon: I'm glad to hear that! Motivation is everything.
Barbara: Sure. He emphasized the importance of teamwork. He said he would call a meeting soon to talk about the project in detail.
Damon: Sounds good. I think the sooner we have this meeting the better.
Barbara: You can say that again!

DIALOGUE COMPREHENSION 15

1. Barbara hasn't talked to Hank yet.
   True ☐   False ☐
2. Both Barbara and Hank are excited about the new project.
   True ☐   False ☐
3. Hank thinks teamwork is essential.
   True ☐   False ☐
4. Damon thinks it's not necessary to schedule a meeting to talk about the project.
   True ☐   False ☐
5. Both Barbara and Damon agree that the sooner the meeting takes place the better.
   True ☐   False ☐

VOCABULARY & EXPRESSIONS 15

Enlightening = clarifying; making understandable
Yep = yes (informal)
Gung ho = very enthusiastic or excited about something
Contagious = easily spread from one person to another
Teamwork = cooperative work done by a team
Call a meeting = schedule a meeting
You can say that again = you are right; that's true; I agree with you

44

USUAL PHRASES AND QUESTIONS 15

How's the project coming along?
Everything seems to be running smoothly so far
We're ahead of schedule so we should certainly meet the deadline
How was the meeting this morning?
How's the new sales rep doing?
Has the meeting with the sales people been scheduled yet?
Have you had any feedback from customers about the new product yet?
Well done!
Way to go!
My congrats!
Good job!

EXERCISES 15

I – Fill in the blanks below with a word or expression from the *Vocabulary & Expressions* section. Make sure you use the appropriate verb tense.

1. Tim: "Do you like living in the suburbs?"
   Dave: "_____, I just love it. The neighborhood is very quiet and there are lots of green areas. It feels great living here."
2. "It will take _____ to get this project off the ground," said Harry at the meeting.
3. "I'm really _____ about the new project. I do believe we can come up with something interesting and innovative that the market is missing" Luke told a coworker.
4. "Let's _____ to discuss the project in detail," said Ralph.

5. "I learned a lot by attending that seminar. It was really _____," said Ronny to a friend.

45

II – Write the questions you listen to and then choose the right answer.

1. _____?
a. I don't have a clue. I haven't talked to them yet.
b. Really? That's great news.
c. It may take some time for us to do that.
d. They plan to showcase their products at the upcoming fair.

2. _____?
a. Yes sir! I think I can do it.
b. Bill's in charge of marketing.
c. That's what I've been trained for.
d. No, not yet.

3. _____?
a. Sure, if you think so go ahead!
b. Yep, I talked to him in the morning. He seems to be really interested in our products.
c. Yep, that's what he told me.
d. I think so. I'll find out more about it tomorrow.

4. _____?
a. No, I haven't heard about it yet.
b. Dave's in charge of the shipping department.
c. We're doing fine sir. Everything's running smoothly and we're ahead of schedule.
d. We're going bicycle riding tomorrow. Would you like to come along with us?

5. _____?
a. Sure, I'll let you know as soon as I have any more news.
b. Yeah, I posted something new on the blog today.
c. Who knows? Let's see how it goes.
d. That's an interesting post. Have you read it yet?

III – Look at the answers and ask questions using the cues provided between parentheses.

1. (new secretary/ doing)
You: _____?
Josh: She's doing very well.

2. (the meeting/ yesterday)
You: _____?
Barry: It was very productive indeed.

3. (in charge of/ logistics)
You: _____?
Heather: Paul is and he's really good at it.

4. (congrats/ do a great job)
You: _____!
Bill: Thanks! I appreciate it.

5. (project/ come along)
You: _____?
Linda: We're doing OK. We're actually ahead of schedule.

UNIT 16
PEDINDO FAVORES

46
DIALOGUE 16
DO YOU THINK YOU COULD DO ME A HUGE FAVOR?
Jeff: Hey Chuck, do you think you could do me a huge favor?
Chuck: I hope so. What do you need?
Jeff: Well, this is kind of awkward, but I ran out of money and I need to borrow some.
Chuck: How much do you need?
Jeff: One grand, I'm afraid.
Chuck: One thousand dollars? Wow Jeff, I'm sorry, but I just don't have that kind of cash on me right now.
Jeff: Yeah, I know. I didn't expect you would. Do you think you could withdraw money at the ATM in the drugstore nearby?
Chuck: Uh, well, I guess, but I keep all my money invested. Maybe I could lend you fifty bucks for now. Would that help?
Jeff: Fifty bucks? Yeah, I guess that's better than nothing. Thanks a million Chuck! I'll get my paycheck in a few days and then I'll pay you back.
Chuck: OK Jeff, no worries!

DIALOGUE COMPREHENSION 16
1. Chuck is not surprised that Jeff needs to borrow one thousand dollars.
   True ☐   False ☐
2. Jeff asks Chuck for a big favor.
   True ☐   False ☐

3. Chuck can only lend Jeff fifty dollars.
   True ☐ False ☐
4. Jeff explains to Chuck why he needs one thousand dollars.
   True ☐ False ☐
5. Jeff intends to pay Chuck back in a few days.
   True ☐ False ☐

VOCABULARY & EXPRESSIONS 16

Huge = very big; enormous
Awkward = embarrassing
Grand = one thousand dollars
Withdraw = take money from a bank account
ATM = automated teller machine
Buck = dollar
Paycheck = a bank check given as salary
Thanks a million! = thank you very much
Pay back = pay money owed to someone
No worries = no problem; don't worry

47

USUAL PHRASES AND QUESTIONS 16

How much did you spend on that shirt/ tie?
Do you know if there's an ATM around here?
Can you lend me some cash?
Sure, how much do you need?
I borrowed forty bucks from Mike and I need to pay him back today.
How much do I owe you?
Six bucks for a cappuccino? That's a rip-off!
Those sneakers were dirt cheap.
What's the currency in Canada?
It's the Canadian dollar
Can I pay you back tomorrow?
You can pay in cash, by check or make a wire transfer
I had to withdraw money from my account to make some payments

EXERCISES 16

I – Fill in the blanks below with a word or expression from the *Vocabulary & Expressions* section. Make sure you use the appropriate verb tense.

1. "I need to go to an _____ to _____ some cash."
2. "I don't know how to put this. I'm in an _____ situation. I think I need your help," said Brian to a friend.
3. Kate lives in a _____ house. It's got seven bedrooms, a spacious living room, a big kitchen and dining room and several bathrooms.
4. "I spent five _____ on that second-hand car," Josh told Luke.
5. "Can you lend me twenty _____ ? I'll _____ you _____ tomorrow," Gregory asked a friend.

48 🎧

II – Write the questions you listen to and then choose the right answer.

1. _____?
a. I need to get some cash at the ATM.
b. That's the one, thanks!
c. Yeah, that's right.
d. There's one in that drugstore across the street.

2. _____?
a. I'll need to lend him one grand.
b. Around three grand.
c. I think so.
d. I'd lend him some cash if I were you.

3. _____?
a. Sorry, I'm flat broke. I don't have any money on me now.
b. Twenty bucks will do.
c. I sure need some cash.
d. Sorry, I don't think it's worth that much.

4. _____?
a. That's right. It's a brand-new suit.
b. I do have a black suit.
c. Three hundred bucks. It was on sale!
d. I spent about ten minutes to get there.

5. _____?
a. Yes, I've already been to Australia.
b. The capital of Australia? It's Canberra.
c. It's the Canadian dollar.
d. It's the Australian dollar.

III – Look at the answers and ask questions using the cues provided between parentheses.

1. (how much/ owe you)
You: _____?
Terry: Twenty-five bucks.

2. (currency/ England)
You: _____?
Sheila: It's the pound.

3. (lend/ some money)
You: _____?
Ralph: How much do you need?

4. (how much/ spend/ that new bicycle)
You: _____?
Dick: $500. It's an aluminum one, it's very light.

5. (pay back/ tomorrow)
You: _____?
Neil: Sure, no problem!

UNIT 17
UMA CONSULTA AO DENTISTA

49

DIALOGUE 17
A DENTAL APPOINTMENT

Hank: I have to get going now. I'll see you later.
Fred: Where are you off to in such a hurry?
Hank: I have a dental appointment and I don't want to be late.
Fred: A dental appointment? Gosh, I can't remember the last time I went to the dentist's.
Hank: Good for you! You probably have great teeth.
Fred: I guess, you know I make sure I always floss and brush them after every meal. So, you think you have a cavity or something?
Hank: I don't have a clue. All I know is I have this tooth that has been bugging me for a while now.
Fred: Yeah, you'd better have it checked. I'll talk to you later then. Good luck at the dentist's!
Hank: Thanks Fred, I'll probably need a little luck. I get terrified when I hear the drill!

DIALOGUE COMPREHENSION 17

1. Hank is in a hurry.
   True ☐   False ☐
2. Fred has been to the dentist recently.
   True ☐   False ☐
3. Hank's dental appointment has been rescheduled.
   True ☐   False ☐

4. Fred takes good care of his teeth.
   True ☐   False ☐
5. Hank is not afraid of going to the dentist.
   True ☐   False ☐

VOCABULARY & EXPRESSIONS 17

Get going = leave
Be off to = be going somewhere
Gosh = interjection used to express surprise or amazement
Floss = use dental floss to clean one's teeth
Cavity = a hole in a tooth
Bug = disturb
Drill = a dentist's tool used for making a hole

50

USUAL PHRASES AND QUESTIONS 17

How often do you brush your teeth?
Do you always floss?
I have a toothache
I have a broken tooth
When was the last time you saw a dentist?
I just panic when I hear the drill
My teeth are very sensitive
Does it hurt here?
My gums hurt
Where can I find toothpaste and toothbrushes?

EXERCISES 17

I – Fill in the blanks below with a word or expression from the *Vocabulary & Expressions* section. Make sure you use the appropriate verb tense.

1. "I hate going to the dentist. The sound of the _____ makes me panic!" Jennifer told Liza.
2. "We'd better _____ . It's getting dark," said Fred to his friends.
3. "I take good care of my teeth. I always _____ and brush them after every meal," Melissa told a friend.

4. "_____, what an awkward situation!" said Dave to a friend with a surprised look on his face.
5. "You told me something was the matter. So, what's _____ you?" Rick asked Bart.

51

II − Write the questions you listen to and then choose the right answer.

1. _____?
a. That's the trouble.
b. He'd like to study dentistry.
c. I think I have a cavity.
d. She's a very good dentist.

2. _____?
a. Sorry, I don't have any dental floss here.
b. Oh, yeah! I always do that.
c. I always drink some coffee after lunch and dinner.
d. That's mouthwash.

3. _____?
a. I think she's a great dentist.
b. My dental appointment has been rescheduled.
c. I make sure I floss after every meal.
d. Not really. Actually I can't remember the last time I saw a dentist.

4. _____?
a. About three times a day.
b. I don't always floss.
c. I have no idea.
d. I have a dental appointment tomorrow.

5. _____?
a. These toothbrushes are more expensive.
b. Aisle five sir.
c. I guess so, let's see!
d. You can find nail clippers in aisle two.

III – Look at the answers and ask questions using the cues provided between parentheses.

1. (I have/ any cavities)
You: _____?
Dentist: Yes, you have two cavities.

2. (often/ brush your teeth)
You: _____?
Dave: Three times a day, after every meal.

3. (hurt/ here)
You: _____?
Patient: Yes, a little.

4. (use dental floss/ regularly)
You: _____?
Nick: I do. Every day.

5. (sell/ toothpaste here)
You: _____?
Drugstore clerk: We do sir. You can find it in aisle six.

UNIT 18
HORA DO JANTAR!

52

DIALOGUE 18
GETTING THINGS READY FOR DINNER.

Matt: What are you doing honey?
Celine: I'm peeling some oranges. I want to make a fruit salad for dessert.
Matt: Great idea. Wow, those strawberries look yummy!
Celine: And they are ripe too. I just had some now. They taste delicious.
Matt: I bet they do. Do you need any help?
Celine: Uh, yes dear. Do you think you could set the table? Dinner will be ready in a few minutes.
Matt: Sure thing! I'll take care of it. Uhmm, it smells really good. I wonder what you've been cooking.
Celine: You'll find out in a few minutes. Something else honey, I put a bottle of our favorite white wine in the freezer. Maybe you could open it for us?
Matt: I'll do it right away! Wow, you really think of everything, don't you?

DIALOGUE COMPREHENSION 18

1. Celine is getting things ready for dinner.
   True ☐   False ☐
2. Matt had some strawberries just now.
   True ☐   False ☐
3. Celine doesn't need any help.
   True ☐   False ☐

4. Matt is glad to help.
   True ☐ False ☐
5. Celine put a bottle of red wine in the freezer.
   True ☐ False ☐

VOCABULARY & EXPRESSIONS 18
Peel = remove the skin of a fruit or vegetable
Yummy = delicious
Ripe = ready to be eaten
Set the table = place dishes, forks, knives, spoons, glasses etc. on a table before a meal
Sure thing = of course
Find out = discover
Right away = immediately

53 🎧
USUAL PHRASES AND QUESTIONS 18
What do you feel like eating?
Do you like pasta/ chicken/ pancake?
Would you prefer to go out for dinner tonight?
Maybe we could order a pizza
I'm sick and tired of fast food
Can we have a real meal tonight?
I've been eating too much junk food recently
I'd better go on a diet
Does it taste good?
It's delicious
Are you hungry/ thirsty?
This sandwich tastes yucky! What's in it?
Are you a vegetarian?

EXERCISES 18
I – Fill in the blanks below with a word or expression from the *Vocabulary & Expressions* section. Make sure you use the appropriate verb tense.

1. "I have a five o'clock appointment, so I need to leave _____," said Jim to a friend.

2. "So, did you _____ where Monica lives?" Jeff asked Roy.
3. "You'd better _____ those vegetables before you cook them," Carol told Annie.
4. "Uhmmm, this lemon cake is _____ . Did you make it yourself?" Patrick asked Liza.
5. "Can you help me _____ ? The forks, knives and spoons are in the top drawer," Sandy told Joe.

54

II – Write the questions you listen to and then choose the right answer.

1. _____?
a. I'd rather not talk about this now.
b. You'd rather eat something.
c. I don't think so. Let's stay home and order a pizza.
d. Yeah I know, it's delicious.

2. _____?
a. I do. I love pasta.
b. I'd rather not.
c. I would like to.
d. I'd do that if I could.

3. _____?
a. No, I'm not hungry yet.
b. I'm famished.
c. Yes, it is.
d. Yep, can you get me a glass of water please?

4. _____?
a. It looks thick.
b. It sure does. What is it?
c. I think it's pancake
d. No, it isn't.

5. _____?
a. Sure, but I don't feel like cooking. Maybe we could go to a restaurant.
b. They serve real meals there.

c. No, I don't like that kind of food. I'm vegetarian, remember?
d. Let's watch a comedy. I feel like having a good time.

III – Look at the answers and ask questions using the cues provided between parentheses.

1. (you/ hungry)
You: _____?
Jake: Not really. I had a cheeseburger before coming here.

2. (feel like/ eat/ tonight)
You: _____?
Melissa: Maybe some pasta.

3. (help me/ set the table)
You: _____?
Greg: Sure honey!

4. (does it/ taste)
You: _____?
Ben: It tastes good!

5. (like/ some more cake)
You: _____?
Fred: No, thanks! That's enough.

UNIT 19
O FERIADO DE AÇÃO DE GRAÇAS

55

DIALOGUE 19
THANKSGIVING PLANS.

Katrina: So, I heard you're flying to the west coast for Thanksgiving.
Jessica: That's right! I haven't seen my folks in a long time.
Katrina: Do all your siblings still live in L.A.?
Jessica: No, just my younger sister. I have a brother in Denver and a sister who got married to an Italian fashion stylist. They're now living in Milan.
Katrina: You have a sister living in Italy? I guess she's pretty lucky. I've always dreamed of visiting Rome.
Jessica: Really? Who knows maybe we can go to Italy together in the near future. I have to pay my sister a visit, you know.
Katrina: Seriously? That'd be great.
Jessica: What about you? What are you doing for Thanksgiving?
Katrina: I'm staying with my in-laws. We all live in the same neighborhood and that makes things a lot easier for us.
Jessica: Good for you Katrina. Enjoy!

DIALOGUE COMPREHENSION 19

1. Jessica has a sister living in Los Angeles.
    True ☐   False ☐
2. Katrina would rather visit Milan than Rome.
    True ☐   False ☐
3. One of Jessica's sisters is a fashion designer.
    True ☐   False ☐

4. Katrina is spending Thanksgiving with her husband's family.
   True ☐ False ☐
5. Jessica hasn't seen her close relatives recently.
   True ☐ False ☐

VOCABULARY & EXPRESSIONS 19

Thanksgiving = the fourth Thursday in November when American families traditionally have a special meal to celebrate all the things they are grateful for
Folks = someone's close relatives
Sibling = a person's brother or sister
Pay a visit = visit someone
In-laws = someone's spouse's family

56

USUAL PHRASES AND QUESTIONS 19

Do you have any plans for tonight/ the weekend?
What are you doing for Christmas?
Are you traveling on your vacation?
What do you enjoy doing in your free time?
Do you have a hobby?
I enjoy watching movies
I like to go bicycle riding/ go jogging/ go dancing
How about going to the beach this weekend?
What are you planning to do next weekend?
Have you seen your parents/ siblings recently?

EXERCISES 19

I – Fill in the blanks below with a word or expression from the *Vocabulary & Expressions* section. Make sure you use the appropriate verb tense.

1. "I need to _____ my uncle a _____ . I haven't seen him in a long time," said Fred to a friend.
2. Many American families have turkey on _____ Day.
3. "I have two sisters and a brother. How about you? Do you have any _____?"
4. Your spouse's family are your _____ .

5. "My _____ are coming from California to spend Christmas with us," Sabrina told her husband.

57

II – Write the questions you listen to and then choose the right answer.

1. _____?
a. My folks live on the west coast.
b. No, they live in California.
c. They are visiting you tomorrow.
d. Unfortunately not this year. Maybe next year.

2. _____?
a. No, thanks, I'm OK.
b. I used to collect stamps when I was a teenager, but I don't have time for that now.
c. That's your hobby, right?
d. I do, I go there every Friday.

3. _____?
a. I do, I feel like swimming today.
b. I did, the weather was really good.
c. I will talk to them about that in the afternoon.
d. I'm starving. I need to go grab a bite to eat somewhere.

4. _____?
a. We often go bicycle riding together.
b. Yes, he has a brand-new bicycle.
c. About three times a week if the weather is good.
d. He might be able to fix your bicycle.

5. _____?
a. I usually do that on Saturday nights.
b. No plans at all, how about you?
c. I'd love to.
d. Maybe, let's see what happens tonight.

III – Look at the answers and ask questions using the cues provided between parentheses.

1. (feel like/ go to the movies tonight)
You: _____?
Daisy: Not really. I'd rather stay home tonight.

2. (go anywhere/ vacation)
You: _____?
Frank: We did. We went to Mexico. It was great, we had a very good time there.

3. (seen/ aunt recently)
You: _____?
Michelle: I have. As a matter of fact I saw her last weekend.

4. (how about/ a drink tonight)
You: _____?
Howard: I appreciate your invite, but I'm really tired. Maybe some other day.

5. (like/ play chess)
You: _____?
Mick: Not really. I find it boring.

UNIT 20
VOCÊ ESTÁ SE SENTINDO MELHOR AGORA?

58

DIALOGUE 20
I REALLY SHOULDN'T HAVE OVEREATEN.
Roy: (sound of car on the road) All these curves on the road are about to make me barf.
Hank: Ok, I'll pull over at the next gas station. I could use a pit stop too, I need to take a leak.
(A few minutes later at the convenience store)
Hank: So, are you feeling any better?
Roy: Yeah, I guess so, but my stomach is aching a little now. I really shouldn't have overeaten at Doug's party.
Hank: I know, I always pig out at barbecue parties too. And those mouth-watering desserts were pretty hard to resist, huh?
Roy: Yeah, I think I'll have a regular coke, it usually helps me digest.
Hank: Sure, I'll have one too.
A few minutes later
Hank: Shall we hit the road?
Roy: Yeah, I can't wait to get home and lie down a little.
Hank: Sure, I could use a nap too pal!

DIALOGUE COMPREHENSION 20

1. Roy is driving.
   True ☐   False ☐
2. Hank needs to use the bathroom.
   True ☐   False ☐
3. Both Roy and Hank have overeaten.
   True ☐   False ☐
4. Hank's stomach is aching a little.
   True ☐   False ☐
5. Roy would like to lie down for a while.
   True ☐   False ☐

VOCABULARY & EXPRESSIONS 20

Barf = throw up; vomit
Pull over = steer a vehicle to the side of the road and stop
Pit stop = a brief stop during a road trip to eat, drink, use the bathroom, rest or refuel
Take a leak = urinate
Overeat = eat too much
Pig out = eat too much; overeat
Mouth-watering = that smells or looks very good
Hit the road = leave a place; go away; begin a journey
Nap = a short sleep, usually during the day
Pal = close friend; buddy

59

USUAL PHRASES AND QUESTIONS 20

I need to sit down/ lie down for a while
Can you open the window please? It's so stuffy in here.
Can I get you anything?
Are you all right?
What's the matter with Joe/ Rita?
Is something the matter?
I feel cold/ hot in here. Can you please turn off/ turn on the air conditioner?
Why is she in such a bad mood?
Can we sit here and rest for a while?

EXERCISES 20

I – Fill in the blanks below with a word or expression from the *Vocabulary & Expressions* section. Make sure you use the appropriate verb tense.

1. "We'd better _____ if we want to get to Houston before it's dark," Ronnie told his friends.
2. "Do you know where the toilet is? I need to _____," Mike asked a friend at the pub.
3. "Hey _____, who's that girl in black over there?" Jake asked his buddy.
4. "I usually take a _____ after lunch on Sundays," Nick told Todd.
5. "Can you _____ please? I'm not feeling well, I think I'm going to _____," said Gregory to the cabbie.

60

II – Write the questions you listen to and then choose the right answer.

1. _____?
a. Fine by me. What about them?
b. It's OK to be OK!
c. Sure, I'm just a little tired.
d. I think that would be OK.

2. _____?
a. You already told me that.
b. I don't have a clue.
c. He went fishing with some friends.
d. He's not that kind of guy.

3. _____?
a. Yeah, that'd be good.
b. I've been doing that for a while.
c. He feels like swimming.
d. I saw him sitting there a while ago.

4. _____?
a. That's a good medicine for headaches.
b. As a matter of fact she does.
c. She has a migraine.
d. She thinks it's not good enough.

5. _____?
a. I'll get you that.
b. I got it!
c. He said something I did not understand.
d. Some water please!

III – Look at the answers and ask questions using the cues provided between parentheses.

1. (turn down/ music)
You: _____?
Dave: Sorry, I didn't mean to disturb you.

2. (you/ all right)
You: _____?
Brenda: I'm OK. I'm just a little sleepy.

3. (feel like/ rest a little)
You: _____?
Tony: I think so. I need to recharge my batteries!

4. (make a pit stop/ next gas station)
You: _____?
Roger: Sure. I could use a pit stop too. I need to stretch my arms and legs and go to the bathroom.

5. (matter/ with Alice)
You: _____?
Suzanne: I think she has a stuffy nose.

UNIT 21
INDO ÀS COMPRAS

61

DIALOGUE 21
SHOPPING AT THE DRUGSTORE.

Ted: Excuse me, do you work here?
Nancy: Yes, sir. How can I help you?
Ted: I'm looking for diapers. Do you know where I can find them?
Nancy: Diapers? Aisle five, this way.
Ted: Thanks, I'm also looking for dental floss and hangers. Where can I find those?
Nancy: Go to aisle four for dental floss and I'm sorry, we do carry hangers, but we're out of them at the moment.
Ted: Ok, no problem. Thanks, you've been very helpful.
Nancy: You're welcome sir.

DIALOGUE COMPREHENSION 21

1. Nancy wasn't helpful at all.
   True ☐   False ☐
2. The drugstore is out of diapers.
   True ☐   False ☐
3. You can find dental floss in aisle four.
   True ☐   False ☐
4. Ted was angry that he couldn't find hangers at the drugstore.
   True ☐   False ☐
5. The drugstore sells hangers, but they're out of them at the moment.
   True ☐   False ☐

VOCABULARY & EXPRESSIONS 21

Diaper = a piece of soft material made of cloth or plastic that a baby wears around its bottom to absorb its urine and excrement
Aisle = a passage between the rows of shelves in a large store or supermarket
Dental floss = thread used to clean the spaces between the teeth
Hanger = a shoulder-shaped frame used for hanging clothes
Carry = have for sale
Be out of = not have
Helpful = providing assistance; useful

62

USUAL PHRASES AND QUESTIONS 21

Where can I find nail clippers/ shampoo/ soap please?
Do you carry diapers/ hangers/ toothbrushes?
What can I do for you?
Can I help you?
I'm looking for short-sleeved shirts/ long-sleeved shirts/ t-shirts
Where's the fitting-room please?
Can I try it on?
Do you have anything on sale?
Everything is 15% off
What size do you wear?
How does it fit?
It's a little tight, I need a larger size please

EXERCISES 21

I – Fill in the blanks below with a word or expression from the *Vocabulary & Expressions* section. Make sure you use the appropriate verb tense.

1. "I don't have enough _____ for all the new shirts I bought. I'll have to buy some tomorrow," said Nick to his wife.
2. "My dentist advised me to use _____ after every meal for cleaning between my teeth," Hank told Ryan.
3. "The attendant told us everything we needed to know. She was very ___ _____ indeed," Maryann told Todd.

4. "Sorry, we _____ sunscreen at the moment. We'll get a supply next Tuesday," the drugstore clerk told Ryan.
5. "Can you change Ronnie's _____ for me honey?" Ralph's wife asked him.

63 🎧

II – Write the questions you listen to and then choose the right answer.

1. _____?
a. We don't carry polo shirts.
b. I don't have a clue.
c. Yes, please, I'm looking for short-sleeved shirts.
d. I do, but that's too small for me.

2. _____?
a. No, that's not my size.
b. Whatever size is fine by me.
c. I'm a good vet.
d. I'm usually a medium.

3. _____?
a. My baby doesn't wear diapers.
b. Yes sir. You can find them in aisle six.
c. I think we need to change his diaper now.
d. They're too heavy to carry.

4. _____?
a. Aisle four ma'am.
b. You have beautiful nails.
c. No, I didn't find them.
d. I'm sure I can find them.

5. _____?
a. He did a lot for me.
b. I can certainly do that.
c. I'm looking for hangers. Do you carry them here?
d. There's a lot I can do for you.

III – Look at the answers and ask questions using the cues provided between parentheses.

1. (anything/ on sale)
You: _____?
Store clerk: We have a special sale on women's shoes today. They are 40% off.

2. (like/ try it on)
You: _____?
Justin: Sure! Where are the fitting-rooms please?

3. (fitting-room/ please)
You: _____?
Store clerk: Back there sir.

4. (have/ that dress in blue)
You: _____?
Store clerk: I think so. Let me check for you.

5. (try on/ smaller size please)
You: _____?
Store clerk: Sure, I'll get it for you.

UNIT 22

NO POSTO DE GASOLINA

64

DIALOGUE 22
FIFTY BUCKS ON PUMP FOUR, PLEASE.
Larry: (sound of car moving) We're running out of gas. I'll pull over at that gas station.
Betsy: Sure honey.
Larry: (sound of car engine turning off, then car door opening and closing) Do you want anything from the convenience store?
Betsy: No sweetie, thanks!
Larry: Ok, I'll be right back.
At the convenience store
Larry: Hi, how's it going?
Convenience store clerk: Pretty good sir. What can I do for you?
Larry: Fifty bucks on pump four, please.
Convenience store clerk: You want premium?
Larry: No, regular please.
Convenience store clerk: Ok, will there be anything else?
Larry: No, that's all, thanks!
Convenience store clerk: Here's your receipt. Have a nice day!
Larry: Thanks!

DIALOGUE COMPREHENSION 22

1. Larry decides to stop by a convenience store to buy a sandwich.
   True ☐ False ☐
2. Betsy pays for the gas.
   True ☐ False ☐

3. The convenience store clerk gives Larry a receipt.
   True ☐   False ☐
4. Larry spends fifty dollars on gas.
   True ☐   False ☐
5. Betsy goes to the convenience store with Larry.
   True ☐   False ☐

VOCABULARY & EXPRESSIONS 22

Run out of = come to an end; not have any left
Pull over = steer a vehicle to the side of the road and stop
Sweetie = dear; sweetheart; honey
Bucks = dollars
Pump = a piece of equipment used to dispense fuel to be sold
Premium = gas that is superior in quality
Receipt = a document that shows that payment has been made

65

USUAL PHRASES AND QUESTIONS 22

We're running out of gas
Do you know if there's a gas station near here?
Can you fill it up while I go to the restroom please?
How can I help you?
Forty dollars/ bucks on pump two please!
Can you check the tires/ oil please?
Can you wash the windshield please?
We'd better leave earlier and avoid the rush hour

EXERCISES 22

I – Fill in the blanks below with a word or expression from the *Vocabulary & Expressions* section. Make sure you use the appropriate verb tense.

1. "Make sure you keep your _____ in case you need to return anything," the store clerk told Mrs. Williams.
2. "You must be starving! I'll fix some pancakes for you _____ . It will just be a minute," Celine told Robin.
3. "I paid only forty-five _____ for this new watch. It was on sale," Greg told Howard.

4. "Thirty dollars on _____ five please," George told the convenience store clerk.
5. "We're _____ sugar. Can you buy some on your way back home _____?" Angela asked her husband.

66

II – Write the questions you listen to and then choose the right answer.

1. _____?
a. So far so good!
b. No, it's not that far.
c. It's pretty reliable.
d. Another ten miles I guess.

2. _____?
a. I got to Boston pretty early.
b. I don't think so. We'd better stop at the next gas station.
c. Don't worry. We always get there on time.
d. We don't have time to stop here now.

3. _____?
a. Seventeen dollars ma'am.
b. I do own a house.
c. As much as possible.
d. Five miles sir.

4. _____?
a. That's the problem.
b. It's pretty cold I guess.
c. I don't have a clue. I'll pull over at the next gas station and check.
d. It doesn't seem so.

5. _____?
a. OK, I'll take care of it.
b. I should probably rest a little.
c. Did you? My congrats!
d. I think I could probably do it if I had a chance.

III – Look at the answers and ask questions using the cues provided between parentheses.

1. (can I/ do for you)
You: _____?
Tim: Twenty bucks on pump five please.

2. (speed limit/ on this road)
You: _____?
Patrick: Fifty-five miles an hour.

3. (running out of/ gas)
You: _____?
Mick: No, the tank is full. I filled it up this morning.

4. (slow down/ please)
You: _____?
Barry: OK, I think there are some bumps ahead.

5. (this/ toll road)
You: _____?
Doug: No, it isn't.

UNIT 23
CHEGA DE BEBIDA POR HOJE!

67

DIALOGUE 23
ENOUGH BOOZE FOR THE DAY.
Jesse: I'm beat. I think I'm turning in early tonight.
Teddy: Me too buddy. That hike in the woods was pretty tiring. My feet are hurting a little, you know. I think my boots are a little tight.
Jesse: Oh, don't worry. I'm sure you'll be feeling better tomorrow. Maybe you're just not used to walking long distances.
Teddy: You're probably right. Hey, do you feel like a nightcap?
Jesse: No, thanks. I've had enough booze for the day. I think I'll put the fishing gear in the pick-up truck now and then I'll hit the sack. Can you give me a hand?
Teddy: Sure Jesse, let's do it!

DIALOGUE COMPREHENSION 23
1. Both Jesse and Teddy feel very tired.
   True ☐   False ☐
2. Teddy has a backache.
   True ☐   False ☐
3. Jesse wants to hit the sack early tonight.
   True ☐   False ☐
4. Teddy feels like a nightcap.
   True ☐   False ☐
5. Jesse puts the fishing gear in the pick-up truck by himself.
   True ☐   False ☐

VOCABULARY & EXPRESSIONS 23

Beat = very tired; exhausted
Turn in = go to bed
Buddy = close friend; pal
Hike = a long walk in the countryside, usually for exercise or pleasure
Woods = an area with trees and other plants, smaller than a forest
Tight = fitting very close to one's body
Nightcap = an alcoholic drink just before bedtime
Booze = alcoholic drink
Fishing gear = equipment used for fishing
Hit the sack = go to bed

68

USUAL PHRASES AND QUESTIONS 23

Do you want to do something tonight?
How about going for a drink after work today?
I'm beat. I just want to go home and get some rest.
Why don't we do something different next weekend?
Do you feel like going camping/ bowling?
How was the party?
Did all your friends show up?
I want to hit the sack early tonight. I need to catch up on my sleep

EXERCISES 23

I – Fill in the blanks below with a word or expression from the *Vocabulary & Expressions* section. Make sure you use the appropriate verb tense.

1. "Can I try on a larger size please? This shirt is a little _____," Joe told the store clerk.
2. "Hey _____, how's it going?" Bill asked Jake as soon as he arrived.
3. "I feel so tired. I think I'll _____ early tonight. I need to catch up on my sleep." said Gordon to his friends.
4. "What a crazy party man! Lots of _____ and fun. We really did have a blast!" Roger told a friend.
5. "I've worked a double shift today and I'm _____. I just want to go home and relax," said Jason to a friend.

69

II – Write the questions you listen to and then choose the right answer.

1. _____?
a. He's a different kind of guy.
b. We try to meet new people every time we go out.
c. She prefers to stay home tonight.
d. Like what? Do you have any ideas?

2. _____?
a. I think she had to stay home and take care of her younger sister.
b. Bill showed up at the party with his new girlfriend.
c. I thought she wasn't coming anymore.
d. I don't want to show up late to work tomorrow.

3. _____?
a. That's not my political party.
b. Great! Very good food and nice people to talk to.
c. It was snowing!
d. We did go to a party last night.

4. _____?
a. I do know where the new bowling alley is.
b. George and Brian went with us.
c. Oh no! I'm too tired for that.
d. Yes, I am.

5. _____?
a. I feel that he's the right guy for the job.
b. I feel cold. Can you turn off the air conditioner?
c. Do you? I don't think so.
d. Maybe we could drop by Fred's place. We haven't seen him in a long time.

III – Look at the answers and ask questions using the cues provided between parentheses.

1. (you/ tired)
You: _____?
Donald: I'm beat! I want to go home and get some sleep.

2. (feel like/ have a drink)
You: _____?
Tony: No, thanks! I've had enough booze for the day.

3. (was/ Fred's housewarming party)
You: _____?
Patricia: It was great! Fred's a great host.

4. (Barry/ did not show up)
You: _____?
Carla: He wasn't invited! That's why.

5. (feel like/ a nightcap)
You: _____?
Ron: Sure, that'd be great!

UNIT 24
ESPORTES AQUÁTICOS

70

DIALOGUE 24
YOU SOUND PRETTY SAVVY WHEN IT COMES TO WATER SPORTS.

Danny: So, what kind of sports are you into Todd?
Todd: I love water sports. Anything to do with water, you name it, I've done it! I must've been a fish in a previous life.
Danny: (laughing) Seriously? You must be a great swimmer then.
Todd: I love swimming. I actually worked as a lifeguard on Malibu beach for a while.
Danny: Really? I bet you saved a few lives there, didn't you? What about scuba diving? Have you ever done it?
Todd: Sure, I have all the scuba diving gear at home. You know, the aqualung, a wetsuit, scuba mask and flippers. By the way, did you know the word scuba is an acronym?
Danny: No, what does it stand for?
Todd: It's short for **s**elf-contained **u**nderwater **b**reathing **a**pparatus.
Danny: Wow Todd! That does make sense. You sound pretty savvy when it comes to water sports. You know, my brother-in-law has a motorboat and a jet ski down in Key Largo. You should come with us next time we go there.
Todd: That would be great. Maybe I can get to show you some of my jet ski tricks!

105

DIALOGUE COMPREHENSION 24

1. Todd seems to be very enthusiastic about water sports.
   True ☐   False ☐
2. Danny knew the word scuba is an acronym that stands for **s**elf-**c**ontained **u**nderwater **b**reathing **a**pparatus.
   True ☐   False ☐
3. Todd likes all kinds of water sports.
   True ☐   False ☐
4. Danny invites Todd to go to Key West.
   True ☐   False ☐
5. Todd doesn't think going to Key Largo is such a good idea.
   True ☐   False ☐

VOCABULARY & EXPRESSIONS 24

Be into = be interested in; like
Lifeguard = person in charge of saving swimmers who are in danger
Gear = special equipment used for a particular activity
Aqualung = a piece of equipment used by divers to breathe under water
Wetsuit = a rubber suit that people wear for water sports
Flippers = a rubber covering for the feet, used in swimming and diving
Acronym = an abbreviation formed by the initial letters that form a word
Stand for = mean; represent
Savvy = well-informed; knowing a lot about something
When it comes to = when the subject is
Trick = a skillful way of doing something performed to entertain people

71
USUAL PHRASES AND QUESTIONS 24

Can you swim well?
How often do you go swimming?
I learned how to swim when I was a pretty young
I just love water sports
Have you ever dived?
Do you like water sports?
I used to play water polo when I was in college
Have you ever been to a water park?

EXERCISES 24

I – Fill in the blanks below with a word or expression from the *Vocabulary & Expressions* section. Make sure you use the appropriate verb tense.

1. "You like rap music, don't you? Did you know that the word 'rap' is an acronym that _____ 'rhythm and poetry'?" Jim asked a friend.
2. "It was fun watching those skateboarders do their _____," said Larry to a friend.
3. "Do you know if there are _____ on duty at this beach?" Ryan asked Jack.
4. "What does the _____ RIP stand for?" Mick asked Jeff.
5. "Grace _____ really _____ vegetarian food. She quit eating meat a few years ago," Brian told a friend.

72

II – Write the questions you listen to and then choose the right answer.

1. _____?
a. I love to go bowling.
b. He's a great diver.
c. About three times a month. I wish I could do it more often.
d. I go to the beach very often in the summer.

2. _____?
a. Not really. I prefer to play basketball and go bicycle riding.
b. He said he hates it.
c. Does she? I didn't know that.
d. I might do that next weekend.

3. _____?
a. Yep, I've been to Mike's diner before.
b. No, I don't drink as much water as I should.
c. Swimming is great. I love it!
d. Just once, but that was a long time ago.

4. _____?
a. That's not Jim's suit. It's mine.
b. Sure, no problem! When do you need it?
c. I don't usually wear a suit to work.
d. It's a bit tight. Do you have a larger one?

5. _____?
a. I lived in Miami for about five years.
b. I like swimming there, they have gorgeous beaches.
c. I often went sky diving. It's a little scary at the beginning, but once you get used to it it's a lot of fun.
d. I did. It's so much hotter there. I often went to the beach.

III – Look at the answers and ask questions using the cues provided between parentheses.

1. (ever been/ water park)
You: _____?
Denise: Not really. I've just been to amusement parks.

2. (CFO/ stand for)
You: _____?
Penelope: It stands for "Chief Financial Officer"

3. (feel like/ go to the beach today)
You: _____?
Rachel: Yep! The weather is great. Let's go!

4. (often/ go swimming)
You: _____?
Brian: Not very often. About once a month.

5. (lifeguard/ on duty at this beach)
You: _____?
Gary: I don't think so. I haven't seen any around.

UNIT 25
ALIMENTAÇÃO SAUDÁVEL

73

DIALOGUE 25
THE BENEFITS OF EATING HEALTHY.

Rita: You really should cut down on the amount of junk food that you've been eating.
Jason: I know, it's just that I can't help it! I love burgers and fries.
Rita: Ok, but can't you change your diet a little? Why don't you try including some veggies and fruit in your daily meals? I think you're just used to burgers and fries, you know, junk food is addictive. Besides it's really fattening and high in calories.
Jason: I should probably do that. Do you think that would help me lose weight?
Rita: Definitely! You will feel a lot better once you start to shed a few pounds.
Jason: Right! I think you've just talked me into starting a new diet from now on. I guess I just have to say goodbye to my beloved burgers.
Rita: Well, you don't have to be radical about it. You should change your diet gradually. I'm sure that you will soon feel the benefits of eating healthy.
Jason: Thanks for the advice Rita! (laughing) I think eating vegetables must be pretty easy for a die-hard vegetarian like yourself!

DIALOGUE COMPREHENSION 25

1. Jason agrees with Rita that he should reduce the amount of junk food that he's been eating.
   True ☐   False ☐
2. According to Rita junk food is not addictive.
   True ☐   False ☐
3. Jason would like to shed a few pounds.
   True ☐   False ☐
4. Rita thinks Jason should change his diet radically.
   True ☐   False ☐
5. Jason is used to eating junk food.
   True ☐   False ☐

VOCABULARY & EXPRESSIONS 25

Cut down = reduce
Junk food = food that tastes good, but has little nutritional value and is high in calories
Can't help it = can't avoid it
Burger = hamburger
Fries = French fries
Veggies = vegetables
Addictive = causing addiction
Fattening = that makes people fat, usually food that is high in calories
Shed a few pounds = lose weight
Talk into = persuade someone to do something
Beloved = a person or something very much liked by someone
Die-hard = someone who is resistant to change

74

USUAL PHRASES AND QUESTIONS 25

What kind of food do you like?
Are you on a diet?
I avoid eating fattening food/ junk food
Do you eat vegetables and fruit every day?
Do you like to cook?
How often do you go to fast food restaurants?
I've been putting on weight in the past few months

I think I'd better go on a diet
Do you drink a lot of soft drinks?

EXERCISES 25

I – Fill in the blanks below with a word or expression from the *Vocabulary & Expressions* section. Make sure you use the appropriate verb tense.

1. "Does the deluxe burger come with _____ on the side?" Barry asked the waitress.
2. "I'd better go on a diet. It would be really good to _____," said Jim to a friend.
3. "Those desserts look very tasty, but they're way too _____. I think I'll just have some coffee," Bill told Norman at the restaurant.
4. "The doctor told me to _____ on the amount of sugar I use every day," Samantha told Neil.
5. "My wife _____ me buying a new suit to go to Kate's wedding," Jason told Nick.

75

II – Write the questions you listen to and then choose the right answer.

1. _____?
a. Not really.
b. He used to, but he doesn't any more.
c. I love chocolate!
d. Yes, I did.

2. _____?
a. Vegetarian food.
b. Sure, let's invite them to the party.
c. It used to be on main street, but I'm not sure if it's still there.
d. That's a great idea. I've been trying to eat healthy recently.

3. _____?
a. My mom loves to make cakes.
b. Yes, he's a great cook.
c. Oh no, I don't have time for that.
d. Not that I know of.

4. _____?
a. Vegetables and fruit are the best really!
b. I'm not on a diet now.
c. Every single day!
d. He loves vegetables.

5. _____?
a. As a matter of fact I have. I cut down on the amount of fast food I used to eat.
b. I do. How about you?
c. I'd rather do that tomorrow.
d. He's very slim. I think he should put on a few pounds.

III – Look at the answers and ask questions using the cues provided between parentheses.

1. (rather/ stay home or go to a restaurant)
You: _____?
Leo: I'd really prefer to stay home tonight. Maybe we could order a pizza.

2. (kind of food/ like)
You: _____?
Ralph: I love pasta and Italian food in general.

3. (can I/ get you)
You: _____?
Tom: Just some coffee and cream please.

4. (like/ a piece of chocolate cake)
You: _____?
Matt: Sure! Did you mom make it?

5. (been/ on a diet)
You: _____?
Louise: Yes, I have. Do you think I look thinner?

UNIT 26
LIGAÇÕES TELEFÔNICAS

76
DIALOGUE 26
WOULD YOU LIKE TO LEAVE A MESSAGE?

Receptionist: (sound of phone ringing) Turner Associates, how can I help you?
Mr. Robbins: Hello! I'd like to talk to Mr. Turner please.
Receptionist: OK sir, hold on a second, I'll put you through to Mr. Turner's secretary.
Hillary: Hello?
Mr. Robbins: Oh, hi, can I talk to Mr. Turner please?
Hillary: Sure sir. May I ask who's calling?
Mr. Robbins: This is Richard Robbins from TGB Warehousing.
Hillary: Just a minute sir, let me see if Mr. Turner is available.
(song ...)
Hillary: Mr. Robbins? I'm sorry. Mr. Turner is talking to someone else on the other line. Would you like to leave a message?
Mr. Robbins: Yes, please. Can you ask him to call me back?
Hillary: Sure sir. I'll do that. Don't worry.
Mr. Robbins: Thanks! Bye.

DIALOGUE COMPREHENSION 26

1. The receptionist transfers Mr. Robbins' call to Mr. Turner.
   True ☐   False ☐
2. Mr. Turner's secretary doesn't seem to be very helpful.
   True ☐   False ☐
3. Richard leaves a message for Mr. Turner.
   True ☐   False ☐
4. Hillary is Richard's secretary.
   True ☐   False ☐
5. Hillary asks Mr. Robbins if he would like to leave a message.
   True ☐   False ☐

VOCABULARY & EXPRESSIONS 26

Hold on = wait
Put through = transfer
Available = free
Hang up = put the receiver back after a telephone conversation
Call back = return the call

77
USUAL PHRASES AND QUESTIONS 26

Hold on a second please...
May I ask who is calling?
Can you speak slowly please?
Would you like to leave a message?
Can you please ask him/ her to call me back?
I'm calling about...
I'm calling on behalf of...
Please don't hang up
What's the area code for New York?
Sorry, I think you have the wrong number

EXERCISES 26

I – Fill in the blanks below with a word or expression from the *Vocabulary & Expressions* section. Make sure you use the appropriate verb tense.

1. "Sorry Jim, I can't talk to you now. Can I _____ you _____?" said Arnold over the phone.
2. "_____ a second please, let me check if Mr. Shields is available now," the secretary told George.
3. "Just a minute ma'am. I'll _____ you _____ to Mr. Miles," Mr. Miles' secretary told Susan.
4. "I'm sorry, but Mrs. Henderson is not _____ at the moment. Would you like to leave a message?"
5. "Please don't _____. I'll try to transfer you to Mr. William's secretary."

78

II – Write the questions you listen to and then choose the right answer.

1. _____?
a. Sure, no problem.
b. I'll probably have to hold on.
c. I did that yesterday.
d. I'm calling on behalf of Mr. Hopper.

2. _____?
a. He's calling me now.
b. This is Carol. Is Joe in?
c. This is really weird.
d. That's right. I called him yesterday.

3. _____?
a. That's the area code for Miami.
b. That's not the area code I'm talking about.
c. I do. It's five miles from here.
d. I have no idea. Why don't you ask Bianca?

4. _____?
a. He left a message on my voicemail.
b. I always leave a message.
c. No, thanks. I'll call back in about half an hour.
d. No, I have to leave early tomorrow.

5. _____?
a. Sure, I'll be in the office in the afternoon.
b. Sure, I'll be on vacation this month.
c. Ok, I'll leave a message on your voicemail.
d. I wish I could call you back later.

III – Look at the answers and ask questions using the cues provided between parentheses.

1. (area code/ for Boston)
You: _____?
Alice: I think it's 617, but let me check and get back to you later.

2. (speak/ slowly please)
You: _____?
Dennis: Sorry, I'll try to.

3. (leave/ a message)
You: _____?
Fred: Yes, please. Can you please ask George to call me back?

4. (I/ help you)
You: _____?
Jake: Hi, I need to talk to Mrs. Smith please.

5. (I ask/ who/ calling please)
You: _____?
Mark: This is Jim. I'm a friend of Harry's.

UNIT 27
ANIMAIS DE ESTIMAÇÃO

79
DIALOGUE 27
I HAVE TO GO FEED MY DOG.

Gus: (sound of dog barking) That guy should keep his dog on a leash.
Tim: You can say that again. You know, I've never believed the saying "barking dogs seldom bite".
Gus: (laughing) Me neither! So you don't have a dog, do you?
Tim: I do! I have a small one. It's still a puppy, it's only one month old. My kids love it.
Gus: Really? Yeah, I think small dogs are OK. What breed is it?
Tim: It's a toy poodle.
Gus: That's a nice one. My next door neighbor has a pit bull. It's so vicious, I often get scared when I see it.
Tim: I can imagine. I don't like big dogs either. Wow, it's a quarter past noon already. I have to go feed my dog. It's probably wagging its tail and waiting for me to come home. Nice talking to you. Take care!
Gus: Same here. Thanks!

DIALOGUE COMPREHENSION 27

1. Tim doesn't like big dogs.
   True ☐   False ☐
2. Gus' neighbor has a pit bull.
   True ☐   False ☐
3. Both Tim and Gus like big dogs.
   True ☐   False ☐
4. Gus believes the saying "barking dogs seldom bite".
   True ☐   False ☐
5. Tim has to go home to feed his dog.
   True ☐   False ☐

VOCABULARY & EXPRESSIONS 27

Leash = a rope used to walk or control a dog or another animal
You can say that again = I agree with you; you are right
Bark = make barking sounds
Bite = use one's teeth to cut or tear
Puppy = a young do; a baby dog
Breed = a particular type of animal
Vicious = extremely violent and dangerous
Scared = frightened
Collar = a band of leather or other material that is placed around an animal's neck
Noon = midday
Feed = give food to
Wag its tail = move its tail from side to side

80 🔊
USUAL PHRASES AND QUESTIONS 27

Do you have any pets?
Who takes care of your dog when you need to travel?
Do you like birds/ cats?
How often do you walk your dog?
Do you feed your cat/ dog/ birds yourself?
What kind of food do you usually give your dog/ cat?
Are you afraid of dogs?

EXERCISES 27

I – Fill in the blanks below with a word or expression from the *Vocabulary & Expressions* section. Make sure you use the appropriate verb tense.

1. "There's no need for you to be _____ . It's just a little _____ ," said Nick to a friend.
2. "Take your _____ dog away from here. I've already told you it gives me the creeps!" Jason told Norman.
3. "I'd never seen a dog like this before. What _____ is it?"
4. Rita grabbed her dog by the _____ and dragged it out of the kitchen.
5. "You see that sign over there? Dogs must be kept on a _____ in this park," Frank told Terry.

81

II – Write the questions you listen to and then choose the right answer.

1. _____?
a. I'm sorry, but I can't. Why don't you ask Laura to take care of them for you?
b. I do! I could've been a vet.
c. I often do that.
d. I could certainly take care of them tomorrow.

2. _____?
a. No, I have just a small dog.
b. No, I don't have any pets.
c. Sure, I think they're nice.
d. Yeah, I'm a little afraid of the big ones.

3. _____?
a. I'd rather have a dog than a cat.
b. I do. I just got a puppy last week. It was a birthday present.
c. Those are my pets.
d. I love dogs and birds.

4. _____?
a. I like to go for a walk in the park.
b. Maybe, I'm not sure.
c. About three times a day.
d. We go there once a week.

5. _____?
a. My best friend's name is Tim.
b. I really think so! Dogs are really loyal.
c. Sure, I have lots of friends.
d. I really think so! You can trust Bill, he's a reliable guy.

III – Look at the answers and ask questions using the cues provided between parentheses.

1. (many pets/ you have)
You: _____?
Tanya: Three. Two cats and a dog.

2. (take care/ dog/ yourself)
You: _____?
Dana: I do. I always feed him and play with him every day. I love my dog!

3. (always had/ a pet)
You: _____?
Johnny: Yep, pretty much so. I got my first puppy when I was just five years old.

4. (whose/ cat/ that)
You: _____?
Teddy: That's Brian's cat.

5. (dog/ wagging its tail)
You: _____?
Gregory: He's happy to see me, that's why! He always does that.

UNIT 28
NO TEATRO

82
DIALOGUE 28
IT'S A GREAT PLAY. IT'S NO WONDER IT GOT SUCH RAVE REVIEWS.

Benny: So, did you like it?
Harold: I loved it! It's a great play. It's no wonder it got such rave reviews.
Benny: Yeah, I think so too.
Harold: I found the performance of that short bald actor particularly brilliant. What's his name again?
Benny: Danny Diller? Yeah, he's a very talented actor.
Harold: So, you're friends with some of the cast members, right?
Benny: Yep, if you stick around I think I can introduce some of them to you.
Harold: Sure, that'd be great!

DIALOGUE COMPREHENSION 28

1. Harold didn't like the play at all.
   True ☐   False ☐
2. The short bald actor's name is Danny Diller.
   True ☐   False ☐
3. Both Harold and Benny think Danny Diller is a bad actor.
   True ☐   False ☐
4. Benny knows some of the cast members.
   True ☐   False ☐
5. Harold is not interested in meeting some of the cast members.
   True ☐   False ☐

VOCABULARY & EXPRESSIONS 28

Rave reviews = enthusiastic reviews
Bald = with little or no hair on the head
Be friends with = have a friendly relationship with
Cast member = an actor/ actress, dancer or singer who performs in a theatrical production, movie or television program
Yep = yes (informal)
Stick around = not go away; stay or wait in a place

83

USUAL PHRASES AND QUESTIONS 28

Have you seen that play yet?
Do you feel like going to the theater tonight?
That'd be great!
What kind of movies do you like?
I love comedies/ thrillers/ action movies/ love stories
I hate dramas/ sci-fi/ westerns
Have you seen the new James Bond movie yet?

EXERCISES 28

I – Fill in the blanks below with a word or expression from the *Vocabulary & Expressions* section. Make sure you use the appropriate verb tense.

1. "Howard introduced me to some of the _____ at the end of the play," said Brenda to a friend.
2. "Gee, I think I'm going _____ . I wonder if there's anything I can do to slow down the process," said Hank to a friend as he looked at himself in the mirror.
3. "Why don't you _____ after class? We could go grab a bite to eat and talk about the chemistry assignment," Ralph told Jason.
4. "I didn't know you were _____ Jake. I thought you hadn't met him yet," Neil told Mike.
5. "How about watching this new movie 'Separate Lives'? It got _____ . Actually one of your favorite actresses works in it," Bill told his wife.

84

II – Write the questions you listen to and then choose the right answer.

1. _____?
a. It sucked!
b. It's at midnight.
c. It was too cold to go swimming yesterday.
d. It's a little tight.

2. _____?
a. I like most kinds, as long as the plot is good, of course!
b. No, I don't.
c. I'd rather stay home.
d. There are many different kinds I believe.

3. _____?
a. He also saw the play.
b. Oh yeah! It was really sunny.
c. She's a great actress.
d. Oh yeah! It was hilarious.

4. _____?
a. I do.
b. I used to go very often, but I rarely go to the movies now. I watch DVDs at home.
c. Do you? I didn't know that.
d. I'll try to.

5. _____?
a. I do. I love going to amusement parks.
b. I'd rather not do that tonight.
c. Not really. I don't usually sleep well at night when I watch thrillers.
d. I didn't.

III – Look at the answers and ask questions using the cues provided between parentheses.

1. (feel like/ go to the movies tonight)
You: _____?
Andrea: Sure! I'd love to see a comedy.

123

2. (like/ the play)
You: _____?
Magda: Not very much. Did you?

3. (rather watch/ a comedy or a thriller tonight)
You: _____?
Fred: I'm too tired to watch a movie. I think I'll hit the sack early tonight. I need to catch up on my sleep.

4. (like/ action movies)
You: _____?
Patty: Not really. I prefer dramas and love stories.

5. (seen/ the new James Bond movie)
You: _____?
Cheryl: Not yet. Have you?

UNIT 29
O NOVO GERENTE REGIONAL

85
DIALOGUE 29
HE STRIKES ME AS A PRO IN WHAT HE DOES.

Chuck: I heard things have been running smoothly since they hired a new regional manager.
Andy: That's right. We can't complain. This new manager strikes me as a pro in what he does.
Chuck: That's good. And how's the head honcho's mood now?
Andy: Much better. You know, we had some difficult months last quarter. We failed to meet the deadline for some of our projects and that really pissed off the boss.
Chuck: I can imagine! He's not exactly someone easy to please, is he?
Andy: No, not really. He can be a tough cookie sometimes. I'm glad things seem to be back on track now.
Chuck: Yeah, sometimes it does take a rainmaker to reverse the situation. It's good to know that things are looking up at your company.
Andy: Thanks Chuck! We still need to see how the next quarters will pan out, but yes, things are way better than before and morale in on the way up.

DIALOGUE COMPREHENSION 29

1. Things are running smoothly now at Andy's company.
   True ☐   False ☐
2. Andy doesn't think the new regional manager is very professional.
   True ☐   False ☐

3. Chuck is glad that things are going well at Andy's company.
   True ☐ False ☐
4. Andy's boss is hard to please.
   True ☐ False ☐
5. Morale at Andy's company is on the way down.
   True ☐ False ☐

VOCABULARY & EXPRESSIONS 29

Running smoothly = going well
Strikes me = seems to me
Pro = professional
Head honcho = boss
Mood = the way someone feels; humor
Meet the deadline = finish something in time
Piss off = make someone angry; annoy
Please = make someone feel happy
Tough cookie = someone who is difficult to deal with
Back on track = running according to schedule again
Rainmaker = someone who makes a lot of money for a company or business
Looking up = getting better; improving
Quarter = a period of three months
Pan out = develop in a particular way
Way better = much better
Morale = the mental or emotional condition of an individual or group
On the way up = increasing

86

USUAL PHRASES AND QUESTIONS 29

I've got a pretty tight schedule today
I'm swamped (with work)
What can we do to boost sales?
We'll need to work overtime to meet the deadline
When do they plan to launch the new product?
Everything is running smoothly at the factory now
Can you brief me on the highlights of the meeting?
Let's call it a day
I badly need a vacation

What does CFO stand for?
How's morale at the company?

EXERCISES 29

I – Fill in the blanks below with a word or expression from the *Vocabulary & Expressions* section. Make sure you use the appropriate verb tense.

1. "I'm not sure I'll be able to go on the fishing trip with you yet. It will all depend on how things _____ , so I'll keep you posted," Hank told Nick.
2. "I'm sure we'll _____ for this project. We are ahead of schedule and things are running smoothly," said Jake at the meeting.
3. "I'm really glad things are _____ at your company. I heard you went beyond all your sales goals last _____ . My congrats!" Luke told a friend.
4. "Martha is very friendly and helpful. Besides that she's always in a good _____ . It's great to have her around really," said Samuel to a friend.
5. "The new _____ is no doubt a _____ . It's really hard to _____ Him," said Harry to a coworker.

87

II – Write the questions you listen to and then choose the right answer.

1. _____?
a. I'll probably hand in the report by Wednesday.
b. Lunch was great. I really like that restaurant.
c. Thanks for inviting me, but I can't. I'm swamped with work so I'll just grab a bite to eat at the company cafeteria.
d. Yeah, she loves taking care of the garden.

2. _____?
a. We all need deadlines, but I don't like them.
b. I think so, but we may need to work overtime.
c. Sure, I liked the project.
d. We'll need to talk about the deadline.

3. _____?
a. He's in Mexico.
b. He's a middle-aged man.
c. Very demanding, but he's very supportive as well.
d. He likes fruits and veggies.

4. _____?
a. I don't think that was said.
b. I don't understand why she's sad.
c. That's what he said.
d. Sure, everything's all set. Don't worry!

5. _____?
a. Sure! I wouldn't miss it for the world.
b. I'd rather check out the new gadgets.
c. He said so, but let me check again please.
d. I did. It was a great talk.

III – Look at the answers and ask questions using the cues provided between parentheses.

1. (CAD/ stand for)
You: _____?
William: It stands for Computer Aided Design.

2. (their market share/ increased recently)
You: _____?
Howard: Yes, by about 12%. I think they're doing a great job.

3. (the commercial/ be broadcast during prime time)
You: _____?
Hank: I don't think they have the budget for that. It's too expensive.

4. (their headquarters/ located)
You: _____?
Brian: In Silicon Valley.

5. (FYI/ stand for)
You: _____?
Olivia: It stands for For Your Information.

UNIT 30
NOVAS EXPERIÊNCIAS

Did you get the hang of it quickly?

Not really.

88

DIALOGUE 30
HAVE YOU EVER DRIVEN A STICK-SHIFT?

Seth: Hey, check out that limo!
Ron: Wow, I'd never seen a stretched limo like that before. It must be kind of awkward driving it, I mean, just imagine how hard it should be to find a parking spot for it.
Seth: Yeah, finding parking space for that size of a limo is definitely a tough task. By the way, have you ever driven a stick shift?
Ron: No, I've never had the chance. Have you?
Seth: As a matter of fact I have. My uncle who lives in Mexico has a stick-shift Beetle. He taught me how to drive it last time I visited him.
Ron: Did you get the hang of it quickly?
Seth: Not really. It took me a long time to get used to it!

DIALOGUE COMPREHENSION 30

1. Seth has a stick-shift car.
   True ☐ False ☐
2. Both Ron and Seth have already driven a stick-shift.
   True ☐ False ☐
3. Ron has already seen a limo before.
   True ☐ False ☐
4. Seth's uncle lives in Mexico.
   True ☐ False ☐
5. Seth thinks parking a stretched limo is not that difficult.
   True ☐ False ☐

VOCABULARY & EXPRESSIONS 30
Limo = a limousine
Awkward = difficult to deal with
Parking spot = parking space
A stick-shift = a car with manual transmission
Beetle = a small round-shaped Volkswagen car
Get the hang of = learn how to do something
GPS = Global Positioning System
Trunk = compartment in a car where you put things such as luggage or shopping
Speedometer = a meter in a vehicle that measures and shows its speed
RV = Recreational Vehicle; a large vehicle where you can sleep, used for traveling
Spare tire = an extra tire carried in a vehicle to be used in case of a flat
ATV = All Terrain Vehicle; a four-wheeler; a vehicle that can travel on rough uneven ground
Tow truck = a truck equipped with winches to pull other vehicles
SUV = Sport Utility Vehicle; a large four-wheel vehicle with two or three rows of seats

89
USUAL PHRASES AND QUESTIONS 30
I'm not used to driving a stick-shift, my car is automatic
Do you know any parking lots near here?
Have you ever driven a truck before?
Can you fly a plane?
We'd better call a mechanic
Can you fix it?
Let's call a tow truck.
We have a flat. Come on, let's get the spare tire.
How often do you have your car washed?
This car runs on gas/ diesel/ ethanol

EXERCISES 30
I – Fill in the blanks below with a word or expression from the *Vocabulary & Expressions* section. Make sure you use the appropriate verb tense.

1. "I've only driven automatic cars so far, so I'm not used to driving a ____, _____" said Barry to a friend.
2. "That was really an _____ situation and to be honest I did not know how I should deal with it," Mick told Gregory.
3. "Learning how to use this new app is no big deal. I'm sure you will ____ _____ it in no time," said Nicholas to a friend.
4. "Looks like we have a flat. Come on, let's get the _____," Ralph told Jefferson.
5. "We rented a car with a big _____ because with had lots of bags," explained Will.

90

II − Write the questions you listen to and then choose the right answer.

1. _____?
a. No, I didn't.
b. He said so, but I'd rather talk to him again, you know.
c. Sure, that's a great road.
d. We'll be stuck in traffic if we leave now. It's the rush hour, remember?

2. _____?
a. It's either right or wrong.
b. That's it.
c. I don't know. It just won't start.
d. It might go wrong.

3. _____?
a. He told me he used to be a truck driver.
b. I don't think so. I've never driven one before.
c. It should be no big deal for Jim.
d. I've seen him drive a truck before.

4. _____?
a. I wish Jerry could fix it.
b. The mechanic said so.
c. At least three days. We don't have the spare part we need here.
d. He'll fix it, don't worry!

5. _____?
a. I don't have a clue. We'd better call a mechanic.
b. That's what seems to be.
c. It seems so.
d. It doesn't seem so.

III – Look at the answers and ask questions using the cues provided between parentheses.

1. (drive/ a stick-shift)
You: _____?
Bill: No, I can't. I've never driven one before.

2. (your car/ run on diesel)
You: _____?
Thomas: No, it doesn't. It runs on gas.

3. (ever been/ in a limo before)
You: _____?
Becky: Not really! Is it comfortable?

4. (ever/ driven an automatic car)
You: _____?
Marco: Yes, I always rent a car when I go to the U.S. and most cars there are automatic.

5. (we park/ here)
You: _____?
Jeff: No, we can't. That's a tow away zone sign there.

RESPOSTAS

UNIT 1
Dialogue Comprehension
1. True   2. False   3. True   4. True   5. False

Exercises 1
I
1. Samantha was **born and bred** in Houston. She's never lived anywhere else.
2. "We had a lot of **fun** at the party last night. There was a band playing live music," said Mike to a friend.
3. "Why don't you ask Fred how to get there? He **knows** this neighborhood **like the back of his hand**."
4. "Wow! Look at that blond girl over there. Isn't she **gorgeous**?", Dave told Brian.
5. "**Let me know** if you need any help with those math exercises. I've already solved them," said Gregory to a classmate.

II
1. Have we met before?
   c. Maybe. You look familiar.
2. Have you met Carol yet?
   c. No, not yet. Can you introduce her to me?
3. Were you born in Denver?
   d. Not really. I grew up in Denver, but I was actually born in Detroit.
4. Come on, I'll introduce you to my sister.
   a. Sure, what's her name?
5. Bill, this is my friend Sheila!
   b. It's nice to meet you Sheila!

III
1. Were you born in Boston?
2. Have you met Sophie yet?
3. Do you like living in Los Angeles?
4. Bill, this is my friend Norma!
5. What do you do for a living?

UNIT 2
Dialogue Comprehension
1. False   2. True   3. False   4. True   5. False

Exercises 2
I
1. Sandy broke up with Ryan because she found out he was **cheating on** her.
2. Franklin **fell in love** with Melissa as soon as he met her. It was **love at first sight**.
3. Greg has been dating Susan for about four years but he thinks he's not ready to **tie the knot** just yet.
4. The **newlyweds** are going to Paris on their **honeymoon**.
5. Nobody expected Jake and Liz to **break up** and call off the **wedding**.

II
1. Do you know why Monica broke up with Josh?
   c. I heard she found out Josh was cheating on her.
2. Is Nick married?
   b. He used to be. He got divorced last year.
3. How long has Jeff been married?
   d. For about two years, I think.
4. Where are the newlyweds spending their honeymoon?
   a. In Italy, that's what I heard.
5. Is Brian still dating Linda?
   c. Not anymore. They broke up a few months ago.

III
1. Why did you break up with Terry?
2. How long have you been married?
3. Where are the newlyweds going for their honeymoon?
4. Is Dana still dating George?
5. What's your boyfriend like?

UNIT 3
Dialogue Comprehension
1. True   2. False   3. True   4. False   5. True

I
1. "We need to **vacuum** the apartment at least once a week because of the dust."
2. "I live with my sister, so we share the **household chores** . I usually clean the house, sweep and mop the floor and my sister does the dishes," said Rhonda to a friend.
3. "Can you smell it? Rita's baking a cake in the **oven** ," Jennifer told Lucy.
4. "Nobody helps me with the housework. I do it all **on my own** ," said Martha to a friend.
5. "Is there any butter left in the **fridge**?" Tim asked his roommate.

II
1. Do you have a favorite household chore?
    a. Are you kidding? I don't have time for housework!
2. Can you take the trash out please? I think it's starting to smell.
    b. Sure, I'll do that right now.
3. Do you iron your shirts yourself?
    d. No, I don't have time for that.
4. Whose turn is it to take the trash out?
    c. I took it the last time, so it's your turn now!
5. How often do you guys clean the apartment?
    a. Not as often as we should. We're both very busy, you know.

III
1. Do you have a maid?
2. What's your favorite household chore?
3. How often do you clean the apartment?
4. Do you like doing housework?
5. Can you help me with the housework?

UNIT 4
Dialogue Comprehension
1. False   2. False   3. False   4. False   5. True

I
1. Make sure you always use the **crosswalk** whenever crossing a street.
2. "You'd better slow down. You can get a **ticket** for going over the speed limit here," Tony advised Nick.

3. We were late to school because of the **traffic jam** on main street this morning.
4. "I need some quarters for the **parking meter**. Do you have any?" Seth asked Hank.
5. "You cannot park here. This is a **tow-away zone**. Look at the sign over there," said Jeff to a friend.

II
1. How can I get to the downtown area by car from here?
   c. Take exit 53 and make a left. You can't miss it.
2. Can you give me directions to the nearest mall?
   d. Sure, I'll show you on the map.
3. I heard you got pulled over by the cops. What happened?
   a. I got distracted and went over the speed limit.
4. Do you have some quarters for the parking meter?
   b. I do. How many do you need?
5. What's the speed limit on this road?
   b. I guess it's fifty-five miles, but I'm not sure.

III
1. How long does it take you to get to school?
2. Can we park here?
3. Is the traffic always heavy?
4. Why did the police stop Frank?
5. Do you have some quarters for the parking meter?

UNIT 5
Dialogue Comprehension
1. False   2. True   3. False   4. True   5. False

Exercises 5
I
1. "I'm going downtown too. Would you like a **ride**?" Seth offered Tim.
2. "Stop **honking**! You're going to wake up the neighbors," Rhonda told her husband in the car.
3. "I have lots of things to do in the office today. I wish someone could **help** me **out**," said Sarah to a coworker.
4. "My daughter is seventeen now. She'll **turn** eighteen on June, 2nd," said Howard to a friend.

5. "If you want a ride just hop in. I'm **headed** that way too," Mike told Rick.

II
1. Would you like a ride downtown?
   b. That'd be great, thanks!
2. Is there a drugstore near here?
   c. Yeah, there's one nearby. I'll show you on the map.
3. Do you know how to get to the park from here?
   a. Not really, but I have a GPS.
4. How can I get to the airport from my hotel?
   d. I don't really know, but if I were you I'd take a cab.
5. Is the mall within walking distance?
   b. Oh yeah. It's very close.

III
1. How far is the airport?
2. Can I get there by subway?
3. Is there a mall near here?
4. Can you tell me how to get to the train station?
5. How far is the park from here?

UNIT 6
Dialogue Comprehension
1. False   2. True   3. True   4. False   5. False

Exercises 6
I
1. "So, what do you **wanna** do tonight? Do you feel like going out?" Richard asked Karen.
2. "I have some quarters, nickels and pennies in my pocket, but I don't have any **dimes**," said Josh to a friend who asked him for ten cents.
3. "I have to go outside for a minute. I forgot to put some coins in the **parking meter**. I'll be right back," Dick told his friends.
4. "Let's have dinner at the new Italian restaurant on main street. **My treat**!" Bob invited Gary.
5. Andy: "Do you have any coins for the parking meter?"
   Bart: "Let me check my pocket. Humm, I only have two quarters and three dimes."
   Andy: "Good, **that'll do**."

II
1. What do you feel like doing tonight honey?
   c. I'm kind of tired, so I'd rather stay home and relax.
2. How about going to the beach this weekend?
   d. Great idea. Maybe we could invite Jeff to come with us.
3. Do you feel like having a drink after work?
   c. I'm sorry, I can't tonight.
4. Do you want to go grab a bite to eat at Ruby's diner?
   a. I'd love that. I'm kind of hungry. Let's go!
5. What would you rather do today?
   b. I need to go shopping for sneakers. I think I'll go to the mall.

III
1. Do you want to go out?
2. How about lunch tomorrow?
3. Do you have some coins for the parking meter?
4. What would you rather do tonight?
5. Did you enjoy the show last night?

UNIT 7
Dialogue Comprehension
1. False   2. True   3. False   4. True   5. False

Exercises 7
I
1. "I'm **famished**. Let's go get something to eat," Dave told Terry.
2. "Hey, you look fatter than the last time I saw you. Have you been **putting on weight**?" George asked Nick.
3. "I'm sick and tired of **fast food**. Can we have a real meal tonight?" said Fred to Samantha.
4. "Would you like to **order** now sir?" the waitress asked Brian.
5. "I really need to **go on a diet**. I'm overweight." Fred told a friend.

II
1. How would you like your steak sir?
   d. Well-done please!
2. What can I get you?
   c. A cheeseburger and fries please.

3. Are you ready to order?
    a. I guess so. What does the grilled chicken come with?
4. Can I get you anything else?
    b. No, thanks. Just the check please.
5. Can you get me another spoon please?
    c. Sure! Just a minute sir, I'll be right back.

III
1. Can you get me a straw please?
2. Are you ready to order?
3. How would you like your steak ma'am?
4. Can I get you anything else?
5. How about dessert?

UNIT 8
Dialogue Comprehension
1. True   2. True   3. False   4. False   5. True

Exercises 8
I
1. Todd: "Do you **feel like** going to the beach this weekend?"
   Rachel: "Sure! It would be great to **lie down** on the sand and **get a tan**."
2. "Come on honey, it's time to get up! I'll **fix** you some breakfast," Hillary told her husband.
3. "You'd better put on some **sunscreen**. Those rays could be harmful to your health," Daisy advised her husband.
4. "Did you hear what the **weatherman** just said? It looks like we're in for a storm," said Doug to a friend.
5. "I'm feeling a little dizzy. I think I'm going to **lie down** for a while," Steph told Nick.

II
1. What would you rather do tonight?
    b. I think I would prefer to stay home and watch a comedy show.
2. What's the weather forecast for the weekend?
    a. It'll be mostly sunny on Saturday, but it might rain a little on Sunday.
3. Would you like to go bowling?
    c. Bowling? Not really. Maybe some other time.

4. Have you ever been to that amusement park
   d. Oh yeah, the rides there are great.
5. What's the weather like today?
   c. It's colder than yesterday. I think you should put on a jacket before going out.

III
1. Do you like to go camping?
2. What's the weather forecast for the weekend?
3. Do you feel like going dancing?
4. Do you want to go to the movies tonight?/ Would you like to go to the movies tonight?
5. What would you rather do today?

UNIT 9
Dialogue Comprehension
1. False   2. True   3. False   4. True   5. True

Exercises 9
I
1. "Our **workload** has practically doubled in the past few months. We badly need to hire some experienced sales reps," Mike told a coworker.
2. "How many employees are **on leave** in your department at the moment?" Mr. Dreyfus asked Mark.
3. "Our boss is sure happy the project is **coming along** fine," said Bill to a coworker.
4. Although they hit a few snags with the project they were still **able to keep things under control** and **meet the deadline**.
5. "So, I heard the shipping department is **short-staffed**. Hasn't HR found anyone qualified yet?" Dennis asked Joe.

II
1. When will they launch the new product?
   c. By mid-September, if everything goes according to schedule.
2. What's the dress code like where you work?
   a. It's very casual. We can pretty much wear whatever we want to.
3. Do you think you will meet the deadline for the current project?
   d. Right now we're behind schedule with the project, so we'll need to work overtime to make sure we meet the deadline.

4. Does your company have an internship program?
   b. Yeah, we have six interns at the moment.
5. Why did the marketing director call off the meeting?
   c. I heard he had a family emergency.

III
1. How many people attended the meeting?
2. What's your e-mail address?
3. How's the project coming along?
4. Does the new rule apply to everyone in the company?
5. Do you get along with your coworkers?

UNIT 10
Dialogue Comprehension
1. True   2. False   3. True   4. True   5. False

Exercises 10
I
1. Betty: "Would you like some cream with your coffee?"
   Matt: "No, thanks! I like it **plain**."
2. One of the **downsides** of being a celebrity is the lack of privacy.
3. "I wish I could have some more of your **yummy** strawberry pie, but I'm on a diet," said Gary to Melinda.
4. "That was a very useful piece of information. Thanks for the **tip**!", Chuck told Larry.
5. "Hummm! This sandwich **tastes** good. What's in it?"

II
1. Can I have some more of your yummy chocolate cake?
   c. Sure, help yourself!
2. Do you want to go grab a bite to eat?
   b. Sure, let's go, I'm starving!
3. What flavor is it?
   d. Vanilla. Humm, it tastes real good!
4. How about some coffee?
   a. No, thanks! I'm OK.
5. What's in that sandwich?
   d. I have no idea, but it tastes really good.

III
1. Would you like some ice tea?
2. Are you hungry?
3. Would you like to go out for dinner?
4. Would you like cream and sugar?/ Do you want cream and sugar?
5. How does it taste?

UNIT 11
Dialogue Comprehension
1. True	2. False	3. False	4. False	5. True

Exercises 11
I
1. Edward is a **brainy** student. He always **scores highly** on all the tests.
2. "What a **tough** test! I left some questions unanswered. Just too difficult," said Roger to a classmate after the test.
3. "What was your **major** in college?" Fred asked Bart.
4. "I'll have to **pull an all-nighter** for the test tomorrow," said Brian to a friend.
5. "Have you done your geography **assignment** yet? We need to hand it in next Tuesday, right?", Jake asked a classmate.

II
1. What was your favorite subject at school?
   d. My favorite subject? History, I've always liked history.
2. Did you get a good score on the test?
   a. I hope so! I'll find out tomorrow.
3. How come you've finished your assignment yet?
   c. I guess I was inspired!
4. Don't you like math?
   b. I hate it!
5. How was the test this morning?
   d. A cinch! I think everyone will get a good score on this one.

III
1. What's your major?
2. Have you done your assignment?
3. Where did you go to high school?
4. Was the test difficult?
5. What's your score?

UNIT 12
Dialogue Comprehension
1. False   2. False   3. True   4. False   5. True

Exercises 12

I
1. "We need to get the heater **up and running**. The winter is coming soon and it will be too cold in here,", said Greg to his roommate.
2. Josh: "Do you want to grab a bite to eat at Joe's diner?"
   Trevor: "**Sounds good**. Let's go!"
3. "You've done a great job. **My congrats**!" Miles told Hank.
4. "Can I leave my **stuff** here?" Dave asked Fred.
5. "Your new apartment looks great and it's really spacious. Do you plan on giving a **housewarming party**?"

II
1. Is the neighborhood where you live quiet? c. Oh yeah, very quiet and I like it that way!
2. Who do you live with? d. I used to live alone, but now my girlfriend has just moved into my apartment.
3. Have you ever lived abroad? a. No, not yet, but I plan to spend some time in Europe.
4. How big is the apartment? b. It's quite spacious. There are three bedrooms, a kitchen, a big living room and a balcony.
5. Have you always lived in an apartment? c. No, I used to live in a big house in the suburbs when I was a teenager.

III
1. How much is the rent?
2. Who do you live with?
3. Do you have good neighbors?
4. Is your apartment big?/ Is the apartment big?
5. How many bedrooms are there?

UNIT 13
Dialogue Comprehension
1. False   2. False   3. True   4. False   5. False

Exercises 13

I
1. "You have the right to be angry, but it's not my fault we missed the deadline, so don't **take it out on me**."
2. "You can definitely count on Jeff. He's very **reliable**."
3. "Can you e-mail me the **spreadsheet** we worked on this morning? I need to check some figures before our meeting with the managers," said Frank to a coworker.
4. "Roger is so **selfish**. He only thinks about himself!" said Brian to a friend.
5. Mike always gets a little **grumpy** when he doesn't have enough sleep.

II
1. What's your sister like?
    d. She's outgoing and talkative. She has a lot of friends.
2. Is she always rude like that?
    b. No, not really, she's usually very friendly.
3. What's the matter with Jim?
    a. I heard he had a heated argument with his girlfriend. That's why he's so grumpy today.
4. Does your twin brother look just like you?
    c. Oh no! We don't really look alike.
5. What does your dad look like?
    b. My dad? He has short black hair and light brown eyes. He's also tall like myself.

III
1. What does Bob look like?
2. What's the matter with Dave?
3. Is Paul always so arrogant like this?
4. What's your boss like?
5. Do you look like your mom or your dad?

UNIT 14
Dialogue Comprehension
1. False   2. True   3. False   4. True   5. False

Exercises 14

I
1. "The last question on the test was a **tough** one. Did you answer it at all?", Jake asked a classmate.
2. "In my opinion he needs professional help. Has he considered seeing a **shrink**?" Jeff asked Brooke.
3. "I think I heard someone **screaming** outside. Let me check what's going on," said Hank to his wife.
4. "Stop **making a scene**. Everyone is looking at us!" Howard told Norma in the restaurant.
5. "You look really tired. Why don't you **take a few days off** and relax?" Doug told a coworker.

II
1. What would you do if you were in my shoes?
   c. I'd tell her the truth.
2. Do you think you could do me a favor?
   a. Sure, what do you need?
3. Can't you try to work things out with her?
   b. I don't think so. She's mad at me like she's never been before.
4. Why don't you take a few days off and relax?
   d. I can't do that now. I have a deadline to meet.
5. What do you think I should do?
   c. Perhaps you should try to talk to them again.

III
1. What would you do if you were in my shoes?
2. Have you tried to talk to her again?
3. What would you advise me to do?
4. Can I ask you something?
5. What do you think I should do?

UNIT 15
Dialogue Comprehension
1. False   2. True   3. True   4. False   5. True

Exercises 15
I
1. Tim: "Do you like living in the suburbs?"

Dave: "**Yep**, I just love it. The neighborhood is very quiet and there are lots of green areas. It feels great living here."
2. "It will take **teamwork** to get this project off the ground," said Harry at the meeting.
3. "I'm really **gung ho** about the new project. I do believe we can come up with something interesting and innovative that the market is missing," Luke told a coworker.
4. "Let's **call a meeting** to discuss the project in detail," said Ralph.
5. "I learned a lot by attending that seminar. It was really **enlightening**," said Ronny to a friend.

II
1. What are our customers saying about the new product?
   a. I don't have a clue. I haven't talked to them yet.
2. Has the meeting with the marketing team been scheduled yet?
   d. No, not yet.
3. Have you talked to that new prospect again?
   b. Yep, I talked to him in the morning. He seems to be really interested in our products.
4. How's the new project coming along?
   c. We're doing fine sir. Everything's running smoothly and we're ahead of schedule.
5. Can you please keep me posted about any further developments?
   a. Sure, I'll let you know as soon as I have any more news.

III
1. How's the new secretary doing?
2. How was the meeting yesterday?
3. Who's in charge of logistics?
4. My congrats! You did a great job!/ Congrats! You've done a great job!
5. How's the project coming along?

UNIT 16
Dialogue Comprehension
1. False   2. True   3. True   4. False   5. True

Exercises 16
I
1. I need to go to an **ATM** to **withdraw** some cash.

2. "I don't know how to put this. I'm in an **awkward** situation. I think I need your help," said Brian to a friend.
3. Kate lives in a **huge** house. It's got seven bedrooms, a spacious living room, a big kitchen and dining room and several bathrooms.
4. "I spent five **grand** on that second-hand car," Josh told Luke.
5. "Can you lend me twenty **bucks**? I'll **pay** you **back** tomorrow," Gregory asked a friend.

II
1. Is there an ATM near here?
    d. There's one in that drugstore across the street.
2. How much money will you need to borrow?
    b. Around three grand.
3. Do you think you can lend me twenty bucks?
    a. Sorry, I'm flat broke. I don't have any money on me now.
4. How much did you spend on that new suit?
    c. Three hundred bucks. It was on sale!
5. What's the currency in Australia?
    d. It's the Australian dollar.

III
1. How much do I owe you?
2. What's the currency in England?
3. Can you lend me some money?
4. How much did you spend on that new bicycle?
5. Can I pay you back tomorrow?

UNIT 17
Dialogue Comprehension
1. True   2. False   3. False   4. True   5. False

Exercises 17
I
1. "I hate going to the dentist. The sound of the **drill** makes me panic!" Jennifer told Liza.
2. "We'd better **get going**. It's getting dark," said Fred to his friends.
3. "I take good care of my teeth. I always **floss** and brush them after every meal," Melissa told a friend.

4. "**Gosh**, what an awkward situation!" said Dave to a friend with a surprised look on his face.
5. "You told me something was the matter. So, what's **bugging** you?" Rick asked Bart.

II
1. What seems to be the problem?
   c. I think I have a cavity.
2. Do you brush your teeth and floss after every meal?
   b. Oh, yeah! I always do that.
3. Have you been to the dentist recently?
   d. Not really. Actually I can't remember the last time I saw a dentist.
4. How often do you brush your teeth?
   a. About three times a day.
5. Where can I find toothpaste and dental floss please?
   b. Aisle five sir.

III
1. Do I have any cavities?
2. How often do you brush your teeth?
3. Does it hurt here?
4. Do you use dental floss regularly?
5. Do you sell toothpaste here?

UNIT 18

Dialogue Comprehension
1. True   2. False   3. False   4. True   5. False

Exercises 18
I
1. "I have a five o'clock appointment, so I need to leave **right away**," said Jim to a friend.
2. "So, did you **find out** where Monica lives?" Jeff asked Roy.
3. "You'd better **peel** those vegetables before you cook them," Carol told Annie.
4. "Uhmmm, this lemon cake is **yummy**. Did you make it yourself?" Patrick asked Liza.
5. "Can you help me **set the table**? The forks, knives and spoons are in the top drawer," Sandy told Joe.

II
1. Would you rather go out for dinner tonight?
    c. I don't think so. Let's stay home and order a pizza.
2. Do you like pasta?
    a. I do. I love pasta.
3. Are you thirsty?
    d. Yep, can you get me a glass of water please?
4. Does it taste good?
    b. It sure does. What is it?
5. Can we have a real meal tonight?
    a. Sure, but I don't feel like cooking. Maybe we could go to a restaurant.

III
1. Are you hungry?
2. What do you feel like eating tonight?
3. Can you help me set the table?
4. How does it taste?
5. Would you like some more cake?

UNIT 19

Dialogue Comprehension

1. True   2. False   3. False   4. True   5. True

Exercises 19

I
1. "I need to **pay** my uncle a **visit**. I haven't seen him in a long time," said Fred to a friend.
2. Many American families have turkey on **Thanksgiving** Day.
3. "I have two sisters and a brother. How about you? Do you have any **siblings**?"
4. Your spouse's family are your **in-laws**.
5. "My folks are coming from California to spend Christmas with us," Sabrina told her husband.

II
1. Are you visiting your folks for Thanksgiving?
    d. Unfortunately not this year. Maybe next year.

2. Do you have a hobby?
   b. I used to collect stamps when I was a teenager, but I don't have time for that now.
3. Do you want to go to the club today?
   a. I do, I feel like swimming today.
4. How often do you go bicycle riding?
   c. About three times a week if the weather is good.
5. What are your plans for tonight?
   b. No plans at all, how about you?

III
1. Do you feel like going to the movies tonight?
2. Did you go anywhere on vacation?
3. Have you seen your aunt recently?
4. How about a drink tonight?
5. Do you like to play chess?

UNIT 20
Dialogue Comprehension
1. False   2. True   3. True   4. False   5. True

Exercises 20
I
1. "We'd better **hit the road** if we want to get to Houston before it's dark," Ronnie told his friends.
2. "Do you know where the toilet is? I need to **take a leak**," Mike asked a friend at the pub.
3. "Hey **pal**, who's that girl in black over there?" Jake asked his buddy.
4. "I usually take a **nap** after lunch on Sundays," Nick told Todd.
5. "Can you **pull over** please? I'm not feeling well, I think I'm going to **barf**," said Gregory to the cabbie.

II
1. Is everything OK?
   c. Sure, I'm just a little tired.
2. Why is Fred in such a bad mood today?
   b. I don't have a clue.
3. Do you feel like sitting here for a while?
   a. Yeah, that'd be good.

4. What's the matter with Rachel?
   c. She has a migraine.
5. Can I get you anything?
   d. Some water please!

III
1. Can you turn down the music?
2. Are you all right?
3. Do you feel like resting a little?
4. Can you make a pit stop at the next gas station?
5. What's the matter with Alice?

UNIT 21
Dialogue Comprehension
1. False   2. False   3. True   4. False   5. True

Exercises 21
I
1. "I don't have enough **hangers** for all the new shirts I bought. I'll have to buy some tomorrow," said Nick to his wife.
2. "My dentist advised me to use **dental floss** after every meal for cleaning between my teeth," Hank told Ryan.
3. "The attendant told us everything we needed to know. She was very **helpful** indeed," Maryann told Todd.
4. "Sorry, we **are out of** sunscreen at the moment. We'll get a supply next Tuesday," the drugstore clerk told Ryan.
5. "Can you change Ronnie's **diaper** for me honey?" Ralph's wife asked him.

II
1. Can I help you at all sir?
   c. Yes, please, I'm looking for short-sleeved shirts.
2. What size do you wear?
   d. I'm usually a medium.
3. Do you carry diapers?
   b. Yes sir. You can find them in aisle six.
4. Excuse me, do you know where I can find nail clippers?
   a. Aisle four ma'am.
5. What can I do for you ma'am?
   c. I'm looking for hangers. Do you carry them here?

III
1. Do you have anything on sale?/Is there anything on sale?
2. Would you like to try it on?
3. Where is the fitting-room please?
4. Do you have that dress in blue?
5. Can I try on a smaller size please?

UNIT 22
Dialogue Comprehension
1. False   2. False   3. True   4. True   5. False

Exercises 22
I
1. "Make sure you keep your **receipt** in case you need to return anything," the store clerk told Mrs. Williams.
2. "You must be starving! I'll fix some pancakes for you, **sweetie**. It will just be a minute," Celine told Robin.
3. "I paid only forty-five **bucks** for this new watch. It was on sale," Greg told Howard.
4. "Thirty dollars on **pump** five please," George told the convenience store clerk.
5. "We're **running out of** sugar. Can you buy some on your way back home **sweetie**?" Angela asked her husband.

II
1. How far is it from here?
   d. Another ten miles I guess.
2. Do we have enough gas to get to Boston?
   b. I don't think so. We'd better stop at the next gas station.
3. How much do I owe you?
   a. Seventeen dollars ma'am.
4. What seems to be the matter?
   c. I don't have a clue. I'll pull over at the next gas station and check.
5. Can you fill it up while I go to the restroom please?
   a. OK, I'll take care of it.

III
1. What can I do for you?
2. What's the speed limit on this road?
3. Are we running out of gas?

4. Can you slow down please?
5. Is this a toll road?

UNIT 23
Dialogue Comprehension
1. True   2. False   3. True   4. True   5. False

Exercises 23
I
1. "Can I try on a larger size please? This shirt is a little **tight**," Joe told the store clerk.
2. "Hey **buddy**, how's it going?" Bill asked Jake as soon as he arrived.
3. "I feel so tired. I think **I'll turn in/ hit the sack** early tonight. I need to catch up on my sleep," said Gordon to his friends.
4. "What a crazy party man! Lots of **booze** and fun. We really did have a blast!" Roger told a friend.
5. "I've worked a double shift today and I'm **beat**. I just want to go home and relax," said Jason to a friend.

II
1. Why don't we do something different tonight?
   d. Like what? Do you have any ideas?
2. Why didn't Melanie show up?
   a. I think she had to stay home and take care of her younger sister.
3. How was the party last night?
   b. Great! Very good food and nice people to talk to.
4. Do you feel like going bowling tonight?
   c. Oh no! I'm too tired for that.
5. So, what do you feel like doing today?
   d. Maybe we could drop by Fred's place. We haven't seen him in a long time.

III
1. Are you tired?/Do you feel tired?
2. Do you feel like having a drink?
3. How was Fred's housewarming party?
4. Why didn't Barry show up?
5. Do you feel like a nightcap?

UNIT 24
Dialogue Comprehension
1. True   2. False   3. True   4. False   5. False

Exercises 24

I
1. "You like rap music, don't you? Did you know that the word 'rap' is an acronym that **stands for** "rhythm and poetry?" Jim asked a friend.
2. "It was fun watching those skateboarders do their **tricks**," said Larry to a friend.
3. "Do you know if there are **lifeguards** on duty at this beach?" Ryan asked Jack.
4. "What does the **acronym** RIP stand for?" Mick asked Jeff.
5. "Grace **is** really **into** vegetarian food. She quit eating meat a few years ago." Brian told a friend.

II
1. How often do you go diving?
   c. About three times a month. I wish I could do it more often.
2. Do you like water sports?
   a. Not really. I prefer to play basketball and go bicycle riding.
3. Have you been to a water park before?
   d. Just once, but that was a long time ago.
4. Do you think you could lend me your wetsuit?
   b. Sure, no problem! When do you need it?
5. Did you use to go swimming a lot when you lived in Miami?
   d. I did. It's so much hotter there. I often went to the beach.

III
1. Have you ever been to a water park?
2. What does CFO stand for?
3. Do you feel like going to the beach today?
4. How often do you go swimming?
5. Is there a lifeguard on duty at this beach?

UNIT 25
Dialogue Comprehension
1. True   2. False   3. True   4. False   5. True

Exercises 25

I
1. "Does the deluxe burger come with **fries** on the side?" Barry asked the waitress.
2. "I'd better go on a diet. It would be really good to **shed a few pounds**" said Jim to a friend.
3. "Those desserts look very tasty, but they're way too **fattening**. I think I'll just have some coffee," Bill told Norman at the restaurant.
4. "The doctor told me to **cut down** on the amount of sugar I use every day" Samantha told Neil.
5. "My wife **talked** me **into** buying a new suit to go to Kate's wedding," Jason told Nick.

II
1. Do you avoid eating any kind of food?
   a. Not really.
2. Do you feel like going to the new vegetarian restaurant on main street?
   d. That's a great idea. I've been trying to eat healthy recently.
3. Do you cook every day?
   c. Oh no, I don't have time for that.
4. How often do you eat vegetables and fruit?
   c. Every single day!
5. You look slim! Have you been on a diet?
   a. As a matter of fact I have. I cut down on the amount of fast food I used to eat.

III
1. Would you rather stay home or go to a restaurant?
2. What kind of food do you like?
3. What can I get you?
4. Would you like a piece of chocolate cake?
5. Have you been on a diet?

UNIT 26
Dialogue Comprehension
1. False   2. False   3. True   4. False   5. True

Exercises 26
I
1. "Sorry Jim, I can't talk to you now. Can I **call** you **back**?" said Arnold over the phone.
2. "**Hold on** a second please, let me check if Mr. Shields is available now," the secretary told George.
3. "Just a minute ma'am. I'll **put** you **through** to Mr. Miles," Mr. Miles' secretary told Susan.
4. "I'm sorry, but Mrs. Henderson is not **available** at the moment. Would you like to leave a message?"
5. "Please don't **hang up**. I'll try to transfer you to Mr. William's secretary."

II
1. Can you hold on a second please?
   a. Sure, no problem.
2. Who's calling please?
   b. This is Carol. Is Joe in?
3. Do you know the area code for Denver?
   d. I have no idea. Why don't you ask Bianca?
4. Would you like to leave a message?
   c. No, thanks. I'll call back in about half an hour.
5. Can I call you back later?
   a. Sure, I'll be in the office in the afternoon.

III
1. What's the area code for Boston?
2. Can you speak slowly please?
3. Would you like to leave a message?
4. Can I help you?/How can I help you?
5. May I ask who's calling please?

UNIT 27
Dialogue Comprehension
1. True   2. True   3. False   4. False   5. True

Exercises 27
I
1. "There's no need for you to be **scared**. It's just a little **puppy**," said Nick to a friend.

2. "Take your **vicious** dog away from here. I've already told you it gives me the creeps!" Jason told Norman.
3. "I'd never seen a dog like this before. What **breed** is it?"
4. Rita grabbed her dog by the **collar** and dragged it out of the kitchen.
5. "You see that sign over there? Dogs must be kept on a **leash** in this park," Frank told Terry.

II
1. You enjoy taking care of pets, don't you?
   b. I do! I could've been a vet.
2. Are you afraid of dogs?
   d. Yeah, I'm a little afraid of the big ones.
3. Do you have any pets?
   b. I do. I just got a puppy last week. It was a birthday present.
4. How often do you walk your dog?
   c. About three times a day.
5. Is a dog really a man's best friend in your opinion?
   b. I really think so! Dogs are really loyal.

III
1. How many pets do you have?
2. Do you take care of your dog yourself?
3. Have you always had a pet?
4. Whose cat is that?
5. Why is your dog wagging its tail?

UNIT 28
Dialogue Comprehension
1. False   2. True   3. False   4. True   5. False

Exercises 28
I
1. "Howard introduced me to some of the **cast members** at the end of the play," said Brenda to a friend.
2. "Gee, I think I'm going **bald.** I wonder if there's anything I can do to slow down the process," said Hank to a friend as he looked at himself in the mirror.
3. "Why don't you **stick around** after class? We could go grab a bite to eat and talk about the chemistry assignment," Ralph told Jason.

4. "I didn't know you were **friends with** Jake. I thought you hadn't met him yet," Neil told Mike.
5. "How about watching this new movie "Separate Lives"? It got **rave reviews**. Actually one of your favorite actresses works in it," Bill told his wife.

II
1. How was the comedy show?
   a. It sucked!
2. What kind of movies do you prefer?
   a. I like most kinds, as long as the plot is good, of course!
3. Did you like the play at all?
   d. Oh yeah! It was hilarious.
4. How often do you go to the movies?
   b. I used to go very often, but I rarely go to the movies now. I watch DVDs at home.
5. Don't you like thrillers?
   c. Not really. I don't usually sleep well at night when I watch thrillers.

III
1. Do you feel like going to the movies tonight?
2. Did you like the play?
3. Would you rather watch a comedy or a thriller tonight?
4. Do you like action movies?
5. Have you seen the new James Bond movie?

UNIT 29
Dialogue Comprehension
1. True   2. False   3. True   4. True   5. False

Exercises 29
I
1. "I'm not sure I'll be able to go on the fishing trip with you yet. It will all depend on how things **pan out**, so I'll keep you posted," Hank told Nick.
2. "I'm sure we'll **meet the deadline** for this project. We are ahead of schedule and things are running smoothly," said Jake at the meeting.
3. "I'm really glad things are **running smoothly** at your company. I heard you went beyond all your sales goals last **quarter**. My congrats!" Luke told a friend.

4. "Martha is very friendly and helpful. Besides that she's always in a good **mood.** It's great to have her around really," said Samuel to a friend.
5. "The new **head honcho** is no doubt a **tough cookie**. It's really hard to **please** him," said Harry to a coworker.

II
1. Do you want to have lunch at Olive Garden today?
    c. Thanks for inviting me, but I can't. I'm swamped with work so I'll just grab a bite to eat at the company cafeteria.
2. Do you think we can meet the deadline for the project?
    b. I think so, but we may need to work overtime.
3. What's the new head honcho like?
    c. Very demanding, but he's very supportive as well.
4. Is everything all set for the presentation tomorrow?
    d. Sure, everything's all set. Don't worry!
5. Are you attending the upcoming tech fair in Houston?
    a. Sure! I wouldn't miss it for the world.

III
1. What does CAD stand for?
2. Has their market share increased recently?
3. Will the commercial be broadcast during prime time?
4. Where is their headquarters located?
5. What does FYI stand for?

UNIT 30
Dialogue Comprehension
1. False   2. False   3. True   4. True   5. False

Exercises 30
I
1. "I've only driven automatic cars so far, so I'm not used to driving a **stick-shift**," said Barry to a friend.
2. "That was really an **awkward** situation and to be honest I did not know how I should deal with it," Mick told Gregory.
3. "Learning how to use this new app is no big deal. I'm sure you will **get the hang of** it in no time," said Nicholas to a friend.
4. "Looks like we have a flat. Come on, let's get the **spare tire**," Ralph told Jefferson.

5. "We rented a car with a big **trunk** because with had lots of bags," explained Will.

II
1. What do you say we hit the road?
    d. We'll be stuck in traffic if we leave now. It's the rush hour, remember?
2. What's wrong?
    c. I don't know. It just won't start.
3. Can you drive a truck?
    b. I don't think so. I've never driven one before.
4. How long will it take you to fix it?
    c. At least three days. We don't have the spare part we need here.
5. What seems to be the problem?
    a. I don't have a clue. We'd better call a mechanic.

III
1. Can you drive a stick-shift?
2. Does your car run on diesel?
3. Have you ever been in a limo before?
4. Have you ever driven an automatic car?
5. Can we park here?

GLOSSÁRIO

A

A cinch: muito fácil; "moleza"; "bico"
A flat: um pneu furado
Abroad: exterior; no exterior; no estrangeiro
Acronym: sigla
Actually: na verdade; na realidade
Addictive: que vicia
Advice: conselho
Advise/ advised/ advised: aconselhar
Ahead of schedule: adiantado; antes do previsto
Aisle: corredor
Amusement park: parque de diversão
Appointment: hora marcada; compromisso
Aqualung: tubo de oxigênio para mergulhadores; aqualung
Area code: código de área
Arrest/ arrested/ arrested: prender
Assignment: tarefa; trabalho escolar
At least: pelo menos
ATM: caixa eletrônico (abreviação de Automated Teller Machine)
Attend/ attended attended: participar (de uma reunião etc.); assistir (a uma aula, uma palestra etc.)
ATV: quadriciclo (abreviação de All Terrain Vehicle)
Available: disponível; disponíveis
Average height: estatura mediana
Avoid/ avoided/ avoided: evitar
Awkward: difícil; complicado; embaraçoso

B

Back on track: de volta aos trilhos
Bad mood: mau humor
Bake/ baked/ baked: assar
Balcony: sacada
Bald: careca
Barbecue: churrasco
Barf/ barfed/ barfed: vomitar
Bark/ barked/ barked: latir
Barking dogs seldom bite: cachorro que late não morde
Be headed: estar a caminho; estar indo
Be off to: estar de saída
Beard: barba
Beat: cansado(a); cansados(as)
Beetle: fusca (carro da marca Volkswagen)
Behind schedule: atrasado(s); atrasada(s)
Beloved: amado(a); amados(as); adorado(a); adorados(as)
Best man: padrinho de casamento
Bet/ bet/ bet: apostar
Bite/ bit/ bitten: morder
Block: quarteirão
Boost/ boosted/ boosted: estimular; aumentar
Booth: estande
Booze: bebida alcoólica
Boring: chato; entediante

Born and bred: nascido e criado
Borrow/ borrowed/ borrowed: pegar emprestado; pedir emprestado
Bottle: garrafa
Bowling alley: pista de boliche
Brainy: inteligente
Brand-new: novinho em folha
Break up/ broke up/ broken up: terminar um relacionamento
Breed: raça de animal
Bride: noiva (no dia do casamento)
Brief/ briefed/ briefed: informar
Broadcast/ broadcast/ broadcast: transmitir um programa de TV ou rádio; ir ao ar
Buck: dólar
Buddy: amigo; amigão; camarada
Budget: orçamento
Bug/ bugged/ bugged: perturbar; incomodar
Bump: lombada; obstáculo
Burger: hambúrguer
Busy: ocupado(s); ocupada(s); movimentado(s); movimentada(s)

C

Cabbie: motorista de táxi; taxista
CAD: programa de computador que facilita a execução de projetos e desenhos técnicos, usado especialmente por arquitetos e engenheiros (abreviação de Computer Aided Design)
Cafeteria: refeitório
Call back/ called back/ called back: retornar a ligação; ligar de volta
Call it a day: dar por encerradas as atividades; terminar
Call off/ called off/ called off: cancelar
Carry/ carried/ carried: estocar; ter disponível para vender
Cast member: membro do elenco
Casual: informal
Catch up on my sleep: colocar o sono em dia
Catch/ caught/ caught: pegar; apanhar (ônibus, metrô, avião, trem)
Cavity: cárie
CFO: diretor financeiro (abreviação de Chief Financial Officer)
Cheat on/ cheated on/ cheated on: trair; ser infiel com o cônjuge
Check: conta de restaurante
Chess: xadrez
Clear up: esclarecer
Clerk: atendente; funcionário(a)
Cloudy: nublado
Coffee maker: cafeteira
Collar: coleira
Come along: progredir
Come along with: vir junto com
Commute: trajeto até o trabalho
Commute/ commuted/ commuted: locomover-se até o trabalho
Competitor: concorrente
Congrats: parabéns
Cook/ cooked/ cooked: cozinhar
Cook: cozinheiro(a)
Cop: policial; "tira"
Core business: atividade principal de uma empresa
Count on: contar com o apoio de alguém

Coworker: colega de trabalho
Cram: estudar intensamente; "rachar de estudar"
Crosswalk: faixa de pedestre
Curly: encaracolado; "enroladinho"
Currency: moeda corrente
Current: atual
Cut down on: reduzir; diminuir; cortar
Cute: bonitinho(a); bonitinhos(as)

D

Dad: pai; papai
Date/ dated/ dated: namorar
Day-off: dia de folga
Deadline: prazo final
Definitely: com certeza; sem dúvida
Deluxe: especial; de luxo
Demanding: exigente(s)
Dental floss: fio dental
Dessert: sobremesa
Diaper: fralda
Die-hard: ultraconservador(a); pessoa que é resistente a mudanças
Digest/ digested/ digested: digerir
Dime: moeda americana de 10 centavos de dólar
Diner: lanchonete
Directions: informações de como chegar a um lugar; instruções
Dirt cheap: muito barato; "de graça"
Dish: prato
Dishwasher: máquina de lavar louça
Disturb/ disturbed/ disturbed: perturbar; incomodar

Dive/ dived/ dived: mergulhar
Diver: mergulhador
Dizzy: tonto(a); tontos(as)
Do the dishes: lavar os pratos
Double shift: turno duplo de trabalho
Downside: desvantagem
Drag/ dragged/ dragged: arrastar
Drawer: gaveta
Dress code: regra de vestimenta
Drill: broca de dentista
Driver's license: carteira de motorista; habilitação
Dryer: secadora
Dump/ dumped/ dumped: abandonar; "dar o fora"
Dust: pó

E

E-mail address: endereço de e-mail
E-mail/ e-mailed/ e-mailed: enviar por e-mail; mandar um e-mail
Engaged: noivo(a) de
Engine: motor
Enlightening: esclarecedor; revelador
Eventually: finalmente; por fim
Exit: saída

F

Fall in love: apaixonar-se
Famished: faminto(a); famintos(as)
Fattening: que engorda
Feasible: possível; praticável
Feed/ fed/ fed: alimentar
Feel like/ felt like/ felt like: sentir vontade de

Figure: algarismo; número
Fill it up: encher o tanque
Find out/ found out/ found out: descobrir; ficar sabendo
Fishing gear: equipamento de pesca
Fishing trip: pescaria
Fit/ fitted/ fitted: servir (roupas, calçados)
Fitting-room: provador
Fix/ fixed/ fixed: consertar; preparar (refeição, lanche etc.)
Flat broke: "sem grana"; "duro"
Flavor: sabor
Flippers: pés de pato
Floss/ flossed/ flossed: usar fio dental; passar fio dental
Fly a plane: pilotar um avião
Folks: pessoas; "pessoal"
Fork: garfo
Freshly squeezed orange juice: suco de laranja feito na hora
Fridge: geladeira
Fries: batatas fritas; fritas
Fun: divertido(a); divertidos(as)
Funny: engraçado(a); engraçados(as)
Furniture: mobília
FYI: para a sua informação (abreviação de For Your Information)

G

Gadget: aparelho eletrônico; "engenhoca"
Gear: equipamento
Gee!: "puxa!"; "nossa!"
Get a tan: pegar um bronzeado; tomar banho de sol; "pegar um bronze"
Get along with: dar-se bem com, ter um bom relacionamento com
Get going: ir andando; ir
Get the hang of: pegar o jeito
Give someone the creeps: deixar alguém tenso ou um pouco assustado
Go ahead!: vá em frente!
Go bowling/ went bowling/ gone bowling: ir jogar boliche
Go jogging: correr
Go on a diet: fazer regime
Go shopping: ir às compras; fazer compras
Goatee: cavanhaque
Gorgeous: muito bonito(a); muito bonitos(as); lindo(a); lindos(as)
Gosh: "nossa"; "puxa"
GPS: GPS (abreviação de Global Positioning System)
Grab a bite (to eat): comer alguma coisa; "fazer uma boquinha"
Grab/ grabbed/ grabbed: agarrar; pegar
Grand: mil dólares
Grass: grama
Groom: noivo (no dia do casamento)
Grow up/ grew up/ grown up: crescer
Grumpy: mal-humorado; rabugento
Gum: gengiva
Gung ho: muito entusiasmado ou animado com algo
Gym: academia de ginástica

H

Hang up: desligar (o telefone)
Hanger: cabide

Harmful: prejudicial
Have a blast: divertir-se muito
Have a clue: ter ideia; saber
Have a good time: divertir-se
Head honcho: chefe
Headquarters: escritório central; sede de uma empresa
Heat/ heated/ heated: esquentar
Heater: aquecedor
Height: altura; estatura
Help out/ helped out/ helped out: ajudar
Help yourself!: sirva-se!
Helpful: útil; prestativo
Highlights: as partes mais importantes ou interessantes de algo; "os pontos altos"
Hike: caminhada
Hilarious: muito engraçado(a); muito engraçados(as); hilário
Hire/ hired/ hired: contratar; empregar
Hit a snag: encontrar um problema ou dificuldade inesperada
Hit the road: ir embora de algum lugar; partir para uma viagem; "pôr o pé na estrada"
Hit the sack: ir dormir
Hold on: esperar
Honey: querido(a); "bem"; "benzinho"; forma carinhosa de chamar a namorada, namorado, marido ou esposa
Honeymoon: lua de mel
Honk/ honked/ honked: buzinar
Hop in: entrar (em um veículo)
Horn: buzina
Host: anfitrião
Household chores: afazeres domésticos; tarefas domésticas

Housewarming party: festa de inauguração de uma casa nova
Housework: serviço doméstico; trabalhos domésticos
Huge: muito grande(s); enorme(s)

I

In a hurry: com pressa
In charge of: responsável por
In no time: em pouco tempo; "rapidinho"
Indeed: realmente; de fato
In-laws: parentes; família (do cônjuge)
Intern: estagiário(a)
Internship program: programa de estágio profissional
Introduce/ introduced/ introduced: apresentar
Invite: convite
Invite/ invited/ invited: convidar
Iron/ ironed/ ironed: passar (roupas)
It's no wonder: não é de admirar

J

Junk food: comida que não é saudável porque contém muita gordura, açúcar etc.; "porcaria"

K

Keep one's fingers crossed: torcer; "fazer figa"
Keep someone posted: manter alguém informado
Kind of: um pouco; "meio"
Knife: faca
Know something like the back of one's hand: conhecer algo como a palma da mão

L

Launch/ launched/ launched: lançar (um novo produto)
Leash: correia; trela (de cachorro)
Lecture: palestra
Let me know: me avise
Let's call it a day: vamos dar por encerradas as atividades; vamos terminar
Lettuce: alface
Lie down/ lay down/ lain down: deitar-se
Lifeguard: salva-vidas
Light: leve(s)
Limo: limusine
Live music: música ao vivo
Long-sleeved shirt: camisa de manga comprida
Looking up: melhorando
Love at first sight: amor à primeira vista

M

Maid: empregada doméstica
Make a left: virar à esquerda
Mall: shopping center
Marital status: estado civil
Mayo: maionese (abreviação de mayonnaise)
Meal: refeição
Meatballs: almôndegas
Medium: tamanho médio; ao ponto (carne)
Middle-aged: de meia idade
Mild: ameno; brando; moderado
Miserable: muito triste
Mop/ mopped/ mopped: esfregar; limpar
Mouth-watering: de dar água na boca
My treat!: é por minha conta!

N

Nearest: o(a) mais próximo(a); os(as) mais próximos(as)
Neighbor: vizinho(a)
Neighborhood: vizinhança; bairro
Newlyweds: recém-casados
Nickel: moeda americana de cinco centavos de dólar
No big deal: fácil; "sem problemas"
No worries!: não se preocupe!; tudo bem!

O

On behalf of: em nome de; no interesse de
On duty: de plantão
On leave: de licença
On one's own: sozinho(a); sozinhos(as)
On sale: em liquidação
On the way up: melhorando; aumentando
Once in a while: de vez em quando
Order/ ordered/ ordered: pedir; fazer o pedido (em restaurante)
Outdoor activities: atividades ao ar livre
Outgoing: extrovertido
Oven: forno
Overeat/ overate/ overeaten: comer demais; "empanturrar-se"
Overweight: acima do peso
Owe/ owed/ owed: dever algo a alguém (dinheiro, favor etc.)

P

Pal: amigo; "camarada"; "chapa"

Pan out: acontecer; desenrolar; evoluir
Panic/ panicked/ panicked: entrar em pânico
Parking meter: parquímetro
Parking spot: vaga; espaço para parar veículo
Pasta: massa (espaguete; lasanha etc.)
Pay a visit: fazer uma visita
Paycheck: cheque de pagamento de salário
Peel/ peeled/ peeled: descascar
Penny: moeda americana de um centavo de dólar
Penthouse: cobertura
Perhaps: talvez
Piece of cake: muito fácil; "moleza"; "bico"
Pig out/ pigged out/ pigged out: comer demais; "empanturrar-se"
Piss off/ pissed off/ pissed off: deixar bravo; irritar; "deixar p. da vida"
Pit stop: pausa em uma viagem de carro para comer, beber, ir ao banheiro, descansar ou reabastecer; "pit stop"
Plain: puro; sem nenhum ingrediente adicional
Play: peça teatral
Please/ pleased/ pleased: agradar
Plot: enredo
Pound: libra esterlina (unidade monetária britânica); libra (unidade de peso)
Premium: gasolina superior em qualidade
Pretty: muito; bastante (usado antes de adjetivos); bonito(a); bonitos(as)
Prime time: horário nobre
Pro: profissional (abreviação de professional)
Prospect: cliente em potencial; "prospect"
Pull an all-nighter: passar a noite estudando ou trabalhando; varar a noite estudando ou trabalhando
Pull over/ pulled over/ pulled over: parar veículo; estacionar
Pump: bomba (de gasolina)
Puppy: cachorrinho; filhote
Put on weight: engordar
Put through: transferir uma ligação telefônica

Q

Quarter: moeda americana de 25 centavos de dólar; trimestre
Quit/ quit/ quit: parar de fazer alguma coisa; largar; deixar; desistir

R

Rainmaker: funcionário influente que atrai bons negócios para a sua empresa; pessoa que "faz acontecer"
Rainy: chuvoso(a); chuvosos(as)
Rap: "rap" (estilo de música)
Rare: malpassado (carne)
Rave review: crítica muito favorável
Receipt: recibo
Recharge/ recharged/ recharged: recarregar
Reliable: confiável; confiáveis

Relish: condimento; molho
Reschedule/ rescheduled/ rescheduled: remarcar (horário; compromisso)
Restroom: banheiro
Ride: carona
Right away: imediatamente
Rink: rinque de patinação
RIP: descanse em paz (abreviação de Rest In Peace)
Ripe: maduro(a); maduros(as)
Rip-off: muito caro; "um roubo"
Role: papel; função; propósito
Roommate: colega de quarto
Rude: mal-educado; rude
Run out of: não ter mais, "ficar sem", acabar (gasolina, tempo, paciência etc.)
Rush hour: hora do rush
RV: trailer (abreviação de Recreational Vehicle)

S

Sales rep: representante de vendas
Sample: amostra
Sand: areia
Savvy: experiente; esperto; competente; bem-informado; entendido
Scared: assustado(a); assustados(as)
Scary: assustador(a); assustadores(as)
Schedule/ scheduled/ scheduled: agendar; marcar horário
Sci-fi: ficção científica (abreviação de Science Fiction)
Score/ scored/ scored: tirar nota; pontuar
Score: pontuação; nota; resultado

Scream/ screamed/ screamed: gritar
Scuba diving: mergulho
Selfish: egoísta(s)
Sensitive: sensível; sensíveis
Set the table: colocar a mesa
Setback: contratempo; revés
Settle in/ settled in/ settled in: estabelecer-se
Share/ shared/ shared: compartilhar; dividir
Shed a few pounds: emagrecer
Shipping department: departamento de expedição
Short-cut: atalho
Short-sleeved shirt: camisa de manga curta
Short-staffed: com um número insuficiente de funcionários
Shout/ shouted/ shouted: gritar
Show up/ showed up/ shown up: aparecer; vir
Showcase/ showcased/ showcased: mostrar a qualidade de algo
Shrink: psicanalista; psicólogo
Shy: tímido(a); tímidos(as)
Sibling: irmão; irmã
Sign: placa
Silicon Valley: Vale do Silício
Size: tamanho
Skateboarder: skatista
Skin: pele
Skip/ skipped/ skipped: pular
Sleepy: sonolento(a); sonolentos(as); com sono
Slim: esbelto(a); esbeltos(as)
Slow down/ slowed down/ slowed down: reduzir a velocidade
Slowly: devagar

Smile/ smiled/ smiled: sorrir
Smoothly: bem, sem problemas ou dificuldades
Sneakers: tênis
Snowy: nevoso; nevado
So far so good: até aqui tudo bem
Soap: sabão
Soft drink: refrigerante
Sounds good: boa ideia
Spacious: espaçoso(a); espaçosos(as)
Spare part: peça de reposição; peça sobressalente
Spare tire: estepe; pneu sobressalente
Speed limit: limite de velocidade
Speedometer: velocímetro
Spitting image: alguém que se parece exatamente como outra pessoa; "a cara de alguém"
Spoon: colher
Spreadsheet: planilha eletrônica
Squeeze/ squeezed/ squeezed: espremer
Stains: manchas
Stamps: selos
Stand for: representar, significar, referindo-se a uma abreviação
Starving: faminto(a); famintos(as)
Steak: bife
Stick around: esperar; ficar por perto
Stick-shift: automóvel com transmissão manual; automóvel com marcha
Storm: tempestade
Stove: fogão
Straw: canudinho
Stretch/ stretched/ stretched: esticar
Stretched: esticado(a); esticados(as)
Strikes me: me parece
Stuff: coisas
Stuffed: satisfeito; "cheio"
Stuffy: abafado
Stuffy nose: nariz entupido
Suit: terno
Sunny: ensolarado
Sunscreen: protetor solar
Supermarket chain: cadeia de supermercados
Supply: fornecimento
Supportive: solidário; compassivo
Sure thing!: claro!; com certeza!
SUV: veículo utilitário esportivo (abreviação de Sport Utility Vehicle)
Swamped with work: cheio de trabalho; "atolado em trabalho"
Sweep the floor: varrer o chão
Sweetie: querido(a); "bem"; "benzinho"; forma carinhosa de chamar a namorada, namorado, marido ou esposa

T

Take a few days off: tirar alguns dias livre do trabalho; tirar alguns dias de férias
Take a leak: urinar; "fazer xixi"
Take a rain check: adiar; "deixar para a próxima"
Take out on: descarregar raiva, mau humor etc. em alguém; "descontar em alguém"
Take turns/ took turns/ taken turns: revezar-se
Talkative: falador(a); que fala muito

Task: tarefa
Taste: gosto; sabor; paladar
Tasty: gostoso; saboroso
Teamwork: trabalho de equipe
Teenager: adolescente
Tent: barraca
Thanksgiving: (dia de) Ação de Graças
Thick: grosso(a); grossos(as)
Thin: magro(a); magros(as)
Thinner: mais magro(a); mais magros(as)
Thriller: suspense
Ticket: multa
Tie the knot: casar-se
Tight: apertado(a); apertados(as)
Tip: dica; informação
Tire: pneu
Tiring: cansativo(a); cansativos(as)
Toll plaza: praça de pedágio
Toll road: estrada pedagiada
Toothache: dor de dente
Toothbrush: escova de dente
Toothpaste: pasta de dente
Tough cookie: pessoa difícil; "durão"
Tough: difícil
Tow truck: guincho
Tow-away zone: proibido estacionar
Toy poodle: poodle toy (raça de cão)
Trade show: feira comercial; feira de negócios
Traffic jam: congestionamento
Trash: lixo
Trick: truque
Trunk: porta-malas
Try on/ tried on/ tried on: experimentar; provar (roupas ou calçados)

Turkey: peru
Turn in/ turned in/ turned in: ir dormir
Turn out fine: acabar bem; "dar tudo certo"
Turn/ turned/ turned: fazer anos ex. turn eighteen (fazer dezoito anos)
Turn: vez ex. it's my turn (é minha vez)
Two-way street: rua de mão dupla

U

Unpack/ unpacked/ unpacked: desempacotar
Unwind/ unwinded/ unwinded: relaxar; descansar
Up and running: funcionando; pronto para usar
Utilities: fornecimento de gás, eletricidade, água ou linha telefônica

V

Vacuum/ vacuumed/ vacuumed: passar o aspirador de pó; aspirar
Vacuum cleaner: aspirador de pó
Vanilla: baunilha
Veggies: legumes
Vet: veterinário(a) (abreviação de "veterinarian")
Vicious: feroz; selvagem

W

Wag/ wagged/ wagged: abanar
Wake up/ woke up/ woken up: despertar; acordar
Wallet: carteira
Warehousing: armazenamento; armazenagem

Washing machine: máquina de lavar roupa
Way better: muito melhor
Way to go!: muito bem!; parabéns!; "é isso aí!"
Weather forecast: previsão do tempo
Weatherman: meteorologista; "homem do tempo"
Wedding: cerimônia de casamento
Weird: estranho(a); estranhos(as)
Well-done: bem passado (carne)
Wetsuit: roupa de mergulho
When it comes to: quando o assunto é; no tocante a
Windshield: parabrisa
Wipe/ wiped/ wiped: limpar; esfregar com pano
Wire transfer: transferência bancária; transferência eletrônica
Withdraw/ withdrew/ withdrawn: sacar; retirar
Woods: floresta; bosque
Work out to: chegar a um valor; totalizar
Work overtime: fazer hora extra
Workload: carga de trabalho
Wow: "uau"; "nossa"

Y

Yep: sim
You can say that again: é verdade; é mesmo; você está certo; concordo plenamente
Yucky: nojento; horrível

SOBRE O AUTOR

José Roberto A. Igreja é graduado em língua e literatura inglesa pela PUC (SP), possui os certificados de proficiência em inglês das universidades americanas BYU – Brigham Young University (Salt Lake City, Utah) e Michigan. Atua no segmento de cursos de inglês *in-company* sendo responsável pelo site www.dialectoenglish.com.br e pelo blog www.faletudoemingles.com.br

É autor de vários livros sobre o idioma inglês, entre os quais *Fale Tudo em Inglês!*, *Inglês Fluente em 30 lições* e *How do you say... in English?*. É também coautor, com Robert C. Young, dos livros *Inglês de Rua – American Slang*, *Fluent Business English*, *Fale inglês como um Americano* e *English for Job Interviews!*, com Joe Bailey Noble III, dos livros *American Idioms!* e *Essential American Idioms*, e com Jonathan T. Hogan, dos livros *600 Phrasal Verbs* e *Essential Phrasal Verbs*, publicados pela Disal Editora.

CONHEÇA TAMBÉM

www.disaleditora.com.br

CONHEÇA TAMBÉM

www.disaleditora.com.br

CONHEÇA TAMBÉM

www.disaleditora.com.br

Este livro foi composto na fonte Thema e impresso em outubro de 2015 pela gráfica Yangraf Gráfica e Editora Ltda., sobre papel offset 90g/m².